JOHN PATRICK BRAY

INCITING incidents

CREATING

YOUR

OWN

THEATRE

FROM

page

TO

performance

Kendall Hunt
publishing company

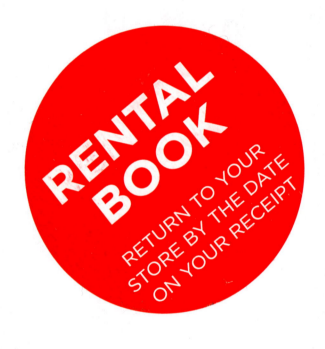

Cover image © Shutterstock, Inc.

www.kendallhunt.com
Send all inquiries to:
4050 Westmark Drive
Dubuque, IA 52004-1840

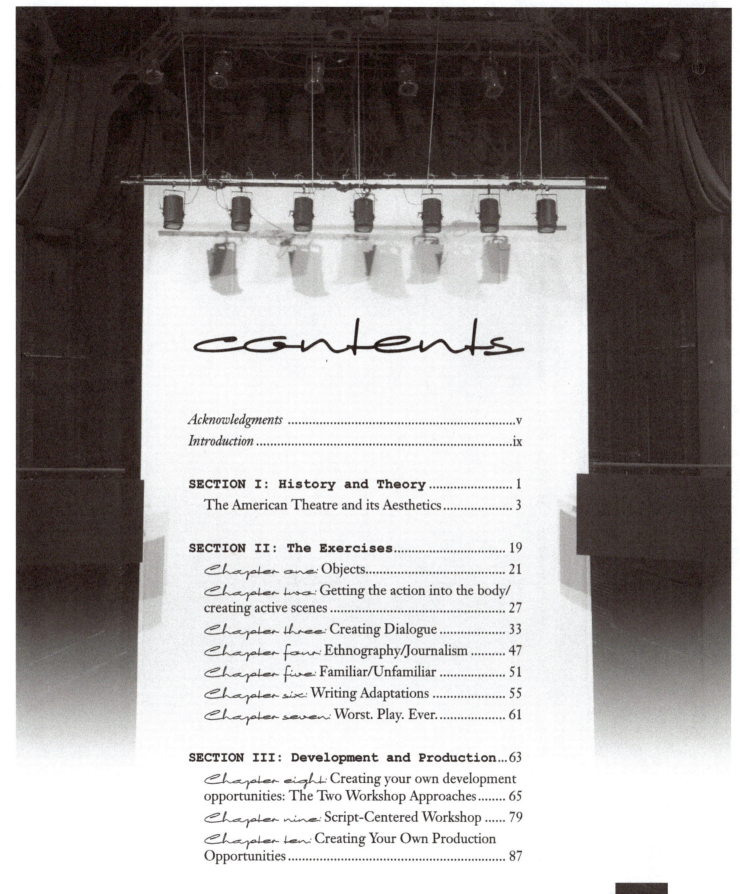

contents

notes

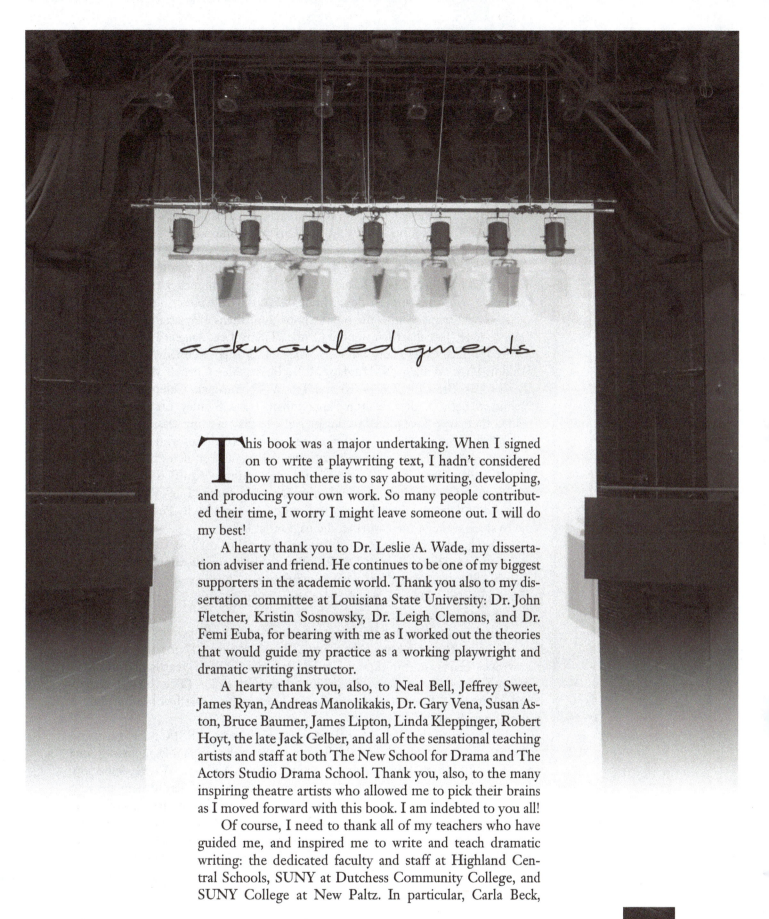

acknowledgments

This book was a major undertaking. When I signed on to write a playwriting text, I hadn't considered how much there is to say about writing, developing, and producing your own work. So many people contributed their time, I worry I might leave someone out. I will do my best!

A hearty thank you to Dr. Leslie A. Wade, my dissertation adviser and friend. He continues to be one of my biggest supporters in the academic world. Thank you also to my dissertation committee at Louisiana State University: Dr. John Fletcher, Kristin Sosnowsky, Dr. Leigh Clemons, and Dr. Femi Euba, for bearing with me as I worked out the theories that would guide my practice as a working playwright and dramatic writing instructor.

A hearty thank you, also, to Neal Bell, Jeffrey Sweet, James Ryan, Andreas Manolikakis, Dr. Gary Vena, Susan Aston, Bruce Baumer, James Lipton, Linda Kleppinger, Robert Hoyt, the late Jack Gelber, and all of the sensational teaching artists and staff at both The New School for Drama and The Actors Studio Drama School. Thank you, also, to the many inspiring theatre artists who allowed me to pick their brains as I moved forward with this book. I am indebted to you all!

Of course, I need to thank all of my teachers who have guided me, and inspired me to write and teach dramatic writing: the dedicated faculty and staff at Highland Central Schools, SUNY at Dutchess Community College, and SUNY College at New Paltz. In particular, Carla Beck,

Elyse Scott, Ken Greenman, Bob Dedrick, Laurence Carr, Mike Weida, Wendy Bohlinger, Dr. Beverly Brumm, Dr. Frank Kratt, and Dr. Joe Paparone.

Thank you to my colleagues in the Department of Theatre and Film Studies for nurturing my growth as a teacher/faculty member: Dr. Antje Ascheid, Mark Callahan, Dr. Marla Carlson, George Contini, Richard Dunham, Dr. Christopher Eaket (a terrific friend), Dr. Freda Scott Giles, Tina Hantula, Mike Hussey, Ivan Ingermann, Dr. John Kundert-Gibbs, Kristin Kundert-Gibbs, T. Anthony Marotta, Dr. Charlie Michael, Dr. Rielle Navitski, Dr. Richard Neupert, Michael O'Connell, Ray Paolino, Julie Ray, Dr. Farley Richmond, Dr. Emily Sahakian, Dr. David Saltz (an incredible Department Head!), Dr. Christopher Sieving, Dr. Fran Teague (my mentor in the Teaching Academy Fellowship Program); and to our staff members Clay Chastain, Steven Carroll, Thomas Stewart, and Dina Canup for your constant can-do! attitude. UGA is a truly inspiring place to work.

A special thank you to the members of the Athens Playwrights' Workshop: George Pate, Jordana Rich, Jennie Czuba, Tifany Lee, Angela Hall, Soudabeh Rafiei, J. Grace Cole, Caity Johnson, Michael "Misha" Kennedy, Jake Watkins, Weldon Pless, William N. Dunlap, Molly Pease, Alex Cornell, Margo Clower, IB Hopkins, Brandon Brown, Kristyl Tift, Will Murdock, Caleb Huett, Grace Nelmes, Robby Nadler, Dalton Sapp, Julian Traas, Stanley Longman, and so many others who have joined us during our Monday evening sessions.

To all of my students—and I need to mention a handful who allowed me to use our summer class together to work the kinks out of some of these exercises: Tony Cerullo, Derek Key, Lawson Chambers, Matthew "Kniff" Kniffen, Stephanie Murphy, Cesar Toledo, Jordan Rothacker, and Lauren "Elle" Woods. Donuts to you all! Additional special thanks to Louise Cook and Molly Pease for allowing me to share some of their work in the pages that follow.

Thank you also to the Rose of Athens artistic director Lisa Cesnik-Ferguson and associate artistic director Danielle Bailey Miller for allowing me to develop their No Shame evenings into a play-reading series. Thank you to Susan Lane for directing my play Donkey, which came out of the program and to Carina McGeehin for supporting our readings.

I also need to mention the generous editors who have seen my plays through to publication: Gene Kato (Next Stage Press), William Demastes (Applause), Lawrence Harbison (Smith and Kraus), Rebecca Ryland (Heartland Plays), JulieAnn Charest Govang (JACPublishing), Van Dirk Fisher (The Riant Theatre), and Martin and Rochelle Denton (Indie Theatre Now). It has been an honor working with you all!

It's thanks to the Rising Sun Performance Company (RSPC) that I can still identify as a working playwright. Thank you to my theatre family, including Akia Squitieri, Elizabeth Burke, Anna Gorman, David Anthony Wayne Anderson, Courtney Hebert, Nancee Moes, and our various friends and family members who joined during our decade-plus together. I must acknowledge our friend, colleague, and brother-in-theatre-arms Nicholas Mevoli, who performed in one of my one-act plays with RSPC for a decade. We lost him in November 2013 when he was attempting a free-diving record. We think of you often and miss you dearly!

A special thanks to Sara M. McGovern and Lauren B. Vondra at the Kendall Hunt Publishing Company for editing and commissioning this book, respectively. Without you, this book would not be possible!

Finally, a big thank you (and hugs!) to my family: my wife, Danielle, who inspires me; my daredevil children, Danny and Sadie, who help me keep everything in perspective; my parents John Newton and Carolyn who insisted I go to college, but never forced a major down my throat; and my brother, Gregory, for your stellar beard, your good looks (we're twins), your camaraderie on *Squeaky Chairs and Blur* (we had a public access movie-reviewing show during high school and college; I'm sure Siskel and Ebert were aware of their stiff competition!) and direction of *Liner Notes*. Many, many thanks to all!

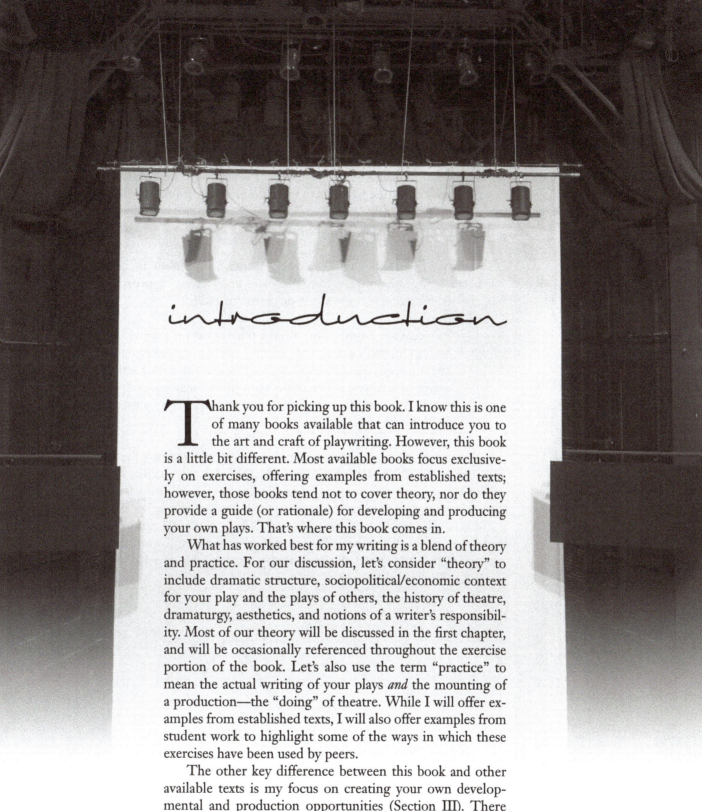

introduction

Thank you for picking up this book. I know this is one of many books available that can introduce you to the art and craft of playwriting. However, this book is a little bit different. Most available books focus exclusively on exercises, offering examples from established texts; however, those books tend not to cover theory, nor do they provide a guide (or rationale) for developing and producing your own plays. That's where this book comes in.

What has worked best for my writing is a blend of theory and practice. For our discussion, let's consider "theory" to include dramatic structure, sociopolitical/economic context for your play and the plays of others, the history of theatre, dramaturgy, aesthetics, and notions of a writer's responsibility. Most of our theory will be discussed in the first chapter, and will be occasionally referenced throughout the exercise portion of the book. Let's also use the term "practice" to mean the actual writing of your plays *and* the mounting of a production—the "doing" of theatre. While I will offer examples from established texts, I will also offer examples from student work to highlight some of the ways in which these exercises have been used by peers.

The other key difference between this book and other available texts is my focus on creating your own developmental and production opportunities (Section III). There has been a sea change in the world of U.S. playwriting with the playwright situating him or herself as artistic director of his or her own work. This shift has been wonderful, as more plays are finding homes, and playwrights are learning how to fully engage with the other disciplines that create our collaborative art of theatre.

Because this book will be used in dramatic writing classes, the tone will sometimes be a bit more formal, particularly when I discuss the history of 20th-century American playwriting. The tone during the exercises will be less formal as I will focus on the nuts-and-bolts of writing. Whether you are enrolled in a dramatic course or reading this book for your own edification, I hope what you will discover is that I am a champion of your work. I want you to find artistic fulfillment in each of your activities, whether writing, developing, or producing your own play.

INCITING INCIDENTS

So, why the title? Let's consider a story. A story has a beginning, middle, and end. When we tell a story, we are using the "once upon a time" approach. You can plug in almost any characters and situations into this model:

> "Once upon a time, there lived a [blank] named [blank]. All was well in [blank]'s world, until [event] happened, thereby destroying the status quo. [Blank] had to act, and do [series of actions] in order to establish a new status quo. [Blank was/was not] able to establish a new status quo, and they all lived [happily ever after/in complete misery]."

In a story, the inciting incident is the moment in which the status quo has changed, and the central character (often called a protagonist, from the Greek term *protagonists*, which means "first speaker," or "one who plays the first character" rather than a chorus member) is forced to act. His or her life has changed, and now they must rectify the situation. There are complications and obstacles, and the story will end with the creation of a new status quo, for better or for worse (depending on whether the protagonist succeeds or not). So, I am borrowing the title from this schema:

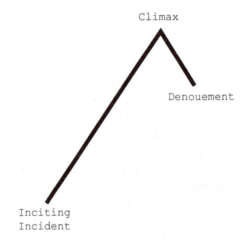

Figure 1. _____

Yes, it's the famous "fish hook" diagram you've seen too many times to count. Sometimes there is a flat line leading up to the inciting incident called the "exposition," which gives us the who, the what, the where, and the why; the background information (often called the "given circumstances"). The climax, or reversal, is where our protagonist will defeat the villain, solve the problem, or where the lovers finally come together. The denouement is the resolution: it's the coda to your story ("and they all lived happily ever after/became zombies").

What I have learned is that we are all very well versed in this approach to story-telling. Almost all of our movies, television shows, and Realistic plays rely on this formula. Rather than focus on this structure, I want to consider the term "incite," and allow that idea to guide our approach to dramatic writing.

From an online dictionary, the term "incite" is defined as "to stir, encourage, or urge on; stimulate or prompt to action," with the example, "to incite a crowd to riot" (Dictionary.com). For the protagonist in this model, incite can be defined as "prompted to act."

Playwrights are attempting to incite an audience to *do*. This gets very complicated. While our desire might be to entertain, our stories also ultimately have a message, so we must be aware of what message we are sending. If we want to reinforce an audience's values, our message should be "keep doing what you are doing." If we want audiences to consider something outside of their own horizon of experiences (which can involve ways to engage with other people, other populations), our message needs to be "try doing something different." Messages that suggest alternatives to an audience's way of engaging the world can make them uncomfortable, and that is really quite okay. For many theatre artists, making an audience uncomfortable is one of their goals. Theatre can get us into some dangerous territory for audiences. There are a number of ways in which writers have tried to engage with both an audience member's thoughts and emotions, with varied results. We will discuss this a bit more fully in Section I.

Finally, it is my hope to incite *you* to build your own theatre community!

WHAT ARE YOU ABOUT TO READ?

Section I features a brief history of the American aesthetic. My reason for including this section is because I am constantly surprised by how many students have not had a theatre history course; either they're putting it off to the last minute, or they are taking dramatic writing as an elective, and therefore don't need a history course to graduate. I think it is vital to understand the context for each script that is written, and how each play is in conversation both with theatrical conventions of the time, as well as the larger world conversations of art, politics, sex, religion, economic differences, social justice, and the hope for a better world. Put another way, our art comes from somewhere. Something has inspired (or incited!) us to write. Let's find out how this impulse inspired writers who laid the path for us.

Section II focuses on exercises I've either learned or developed that have sharpened my skills as a writer. This is where I will talk about the work of established writers, student writers, and some of my own writing. As you work through these exercises, please understand that it is my goal to help you create the experience you wish to concoct for the audience. Early on in my own writing, I would often "get in my own way." These exercises have inspired me and I hope they can inspire you as well.

Section III focuses on ways in which you can create your own development and production opportunities. There are a number of playwright-led development and production companies spearheaded by writers who have wished to find new ways to circumvent the status quo for playwrights, which, in recent years, have included process without production, and limited access to producing theatres (London, Pesner, Voss *Outrageous Fortune*). A number of playwrights who have created their own opportunities have been recognized by the mainstream U.S. theatres, while others have been enjoying their own independent productions, an experience that has its own rewards (as well as networks of like-minded writers).

Portions of Chapter Eight, which focuses on developing your own production opportunities, were originally published in my essay, "Playing Together: How the New York Writers' Bloc Created Camaraderie, Community, and Great Stories" in *Theatre Topics* (Vol. 24 Issue 1, 2014). Portions of Chapter Nine were previously published in *Texas Theatre Journal* (Volume 10, Issue 1, 2014), which is affiliated with the Texas Educational Theatre Association. Finally, portions of Chapter Ten contain parts of my essay, "Playwrights as Auteur, Playwright as Producer: The Economics and Aesthetics of the Twenty-First Century American Playwright," which was originally published in *New England Theatre Journal* (Vol. 23, 2012). I am grateful to *Theatre Topics* editor DJ Hopkins, *Texas Theatre Journal* editor DeAnna Toten Beard, and *New England Theatre Journal* editor Stuart Hecht for granting permission. The reason why I am focusing on self-development-and-production is because I don't want your play to die on the page. A writer's process is only complete when a production has been achieved. Just seeing one of your plays on stage will change the way you think about writing. It is a vital step.

In sum, this book is meant to be used both as a textbook in a dramatic writing class, as well as a guide for those who are already writing. For those already familiar with the theatre and the role of the playwright, feel free to skip ahead to some of the exercises (though I do urge you to look at the section "Internal Logic and Contract with the Audience"), or to the second part of this book where I discuss ways in which you can create your own theatre community. As this is a book for college students, feel free to share these ideas with your peers. See if you can excite them (and incite them!) to build your own collaborative theatre troupe.

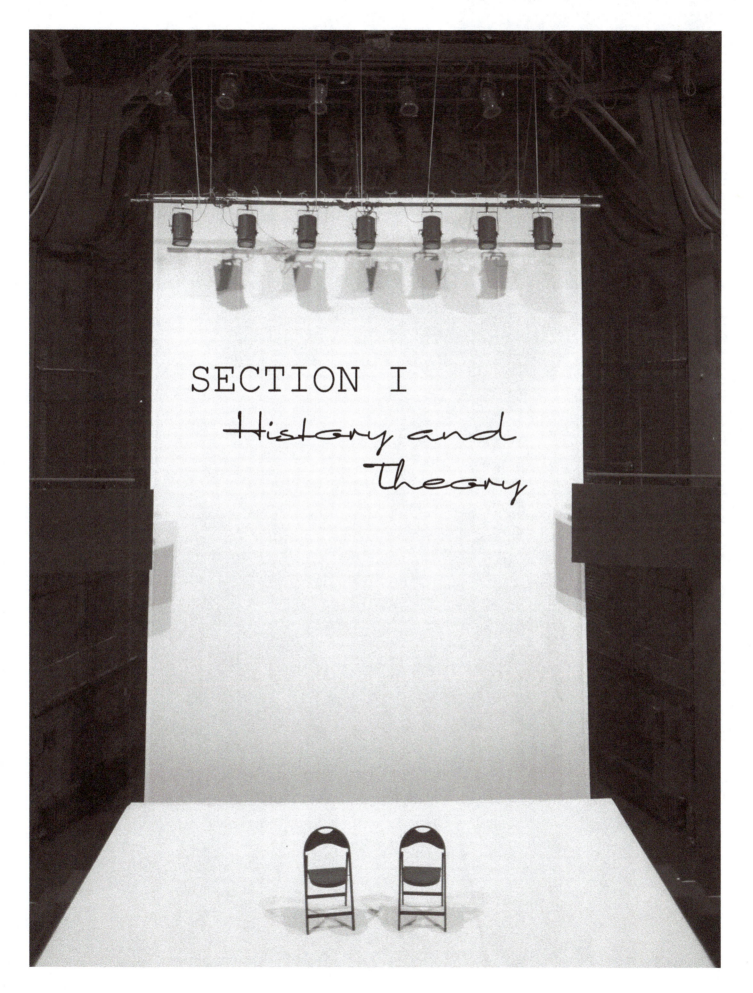

SECTION I

History and Theory

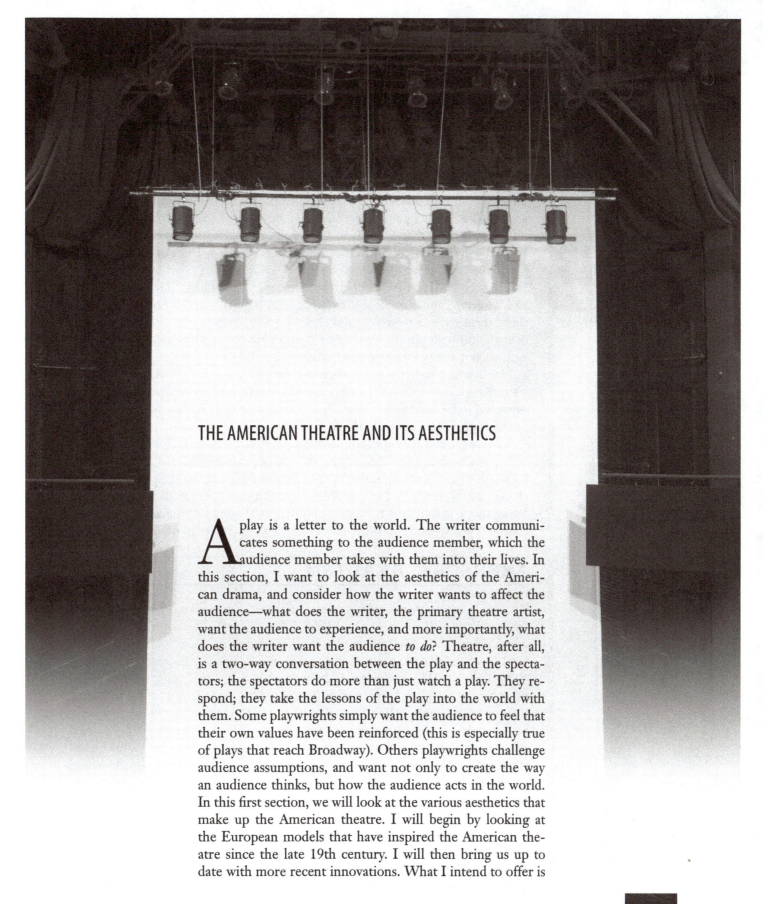

THE AMERICAN THEATRE AND ITS AESTHETICS

A play is a letter to the world. The writer communicates something to the audience member, which the audience member takes with them into their lives. In this section, I want to look at the aesthetics of the American drama, and consider how the writer wants to affect the audience—what does the writer, the primary theatre artist, want the audience to experience, and more importantly, what does the writer want the audience *to do*? Theatre, after all, is a two-way conversation between the play and the spectators; the spectators do more than just watch a play. They respond; they take the lessons of the play into the world with them. Some playwrights simply want the audience to feel that their own values have been reinforced (this is especially true of plays that reach Broadway). Others playwrights challenge audience assumptions, and want not only to create the way an audience thinks, but how the audience acts in the world. In this first section, we will look at the various aesthetics that make up the American theatre. I will begin by looking at the European models that have inspired the American theatre since the late 19th century. I will then bring us up to date with more recent innovations. What I intend to offer is a brief history—as writers, it is important that we know our past. After all, our writing is in conversation with other works of the stage (whether we're aware of it or not). I will begin with a look at Realism, then the historic avant-garde; I will then consider how the 21st century playwright relies on known forms in order to meet or move against audience expectations.

In my Theatre Appreciation course, I usually take two days to talk about the art and craft of playwriting. In the first ten minutes, I differentiate between screenwriting and playwriting. Most students assume that one naturally leads to another (one student, a self-proclaimed stand-up, told me that playwrights were just screenwriters that couldn't make it; I retorted stand-up comics were improvisers that didn't know how to play with others).

If you read Stuart Spencer's excellent *The Playwright's Guidebook*, he suggests that theatre exists somewhere between film and prose, where film is "immediate" and "visceral," and prose is able to "plumb the depths of an experience" (4, 7). In short, theatre serves to give an audience visceral responses, but also relies on a set of analytical skills not required to watch most Hollywood blockbusters (independent and art-house films are another story).

Unlike film and television, theatre is an abstract space. With television and film, the situations that characters are faced with exist in *real time*, and we are supposed to be entirely emotionally involved with the central character: will he or she reach his or her goal? What are the stakes?

There are two points worth mentioning: to some extent, all Western theatre and film is an extension of Realism, which is built on the Judeo-Christian model for storytelling (in an unjust world, one man has the power to bring about positive change for all people, but at a terrible cost to himself). Therefore, when we watch a play, more often than not, we are supposed to become emotionally invested in a central character and his or her quest to achieve a new status quo.

AMERICAN REALISM

Realism, as an aesthetic style, gained prominence in the late 19th century. The earliest plays of Realism, such as Henrik Ibsen's *A Doll House*, were essentially a reworking of the well-made-play model, created by Eugene Scribe. Eugene Scribe's work favored structure over substance, delighting audiences of the early 19th century. He worked with an uncredited team of writers, often referred to as "his factory," in keeping with the assembly-line rhetoric of the Industrial Revolution (Graeme). With the well-made-play, there is an expository first act, a necessary scene, a quid-pro-quo (characters who believe they are talking to each other about something else—only the audience knows that they have a misunderstanding!), a reversal of fortune, and a denouement. There is also usually a prop involved, which signals to the audience that the play is about to end. For example, if I were going to write a well-made-play, I might call it *A Vase of Roses*. My central character would tell a confidant early in Act I, "Oh, I hope no one brings a vase of roses in the room! I'm expecting the queen, and should I see a vase of roses, I should fly into fits! Oh, the embarrassment that would cause!" Close to the end of the play, some character would bring in a vase of roses. Perhaps the queen likes roses; perhaps the person bringing the roses has done so as a result of the quid-pro-quo; whatever the reason, we would have the queen, a vase of roses, and, of course, when the central character enters, the aforementioned fits. In the end, however, wickedness will be punished and our hero will be knighted. These things have to end happily.

The difference with the Realistic plays of Ibsen, is that the last act does not involve a reversal, but, as George Bernard Shaw suggests, a discussion which foregrounds a "social question" (Dukore, 630-631). The discussions at the end of the Realist plays often involved a very present social issue, one that the audience could take with them and consider as they leave the theatre.

Other writers of Realism (and, of course, its cousin Naturalism) created characters that were products of heredity and environment, a way of keeping plays in conversation with the latest theory of evolution as proposed by Charles Darwin. Furthermore, August Strindberg would write a play, *Miss Julie*, that looked closely at the divide between economic classes. Whether or not Strindberg was a reader of Marx, the theories of economics (including the critiques of capitalism) were certainly being discussed across Europe. Writers such as Anton Chekhov gave his characters psychological motivations, in keeping with theories proposed by Sigmund Freud. Characters, therefore, were products of heredity and environment, as well as their economic circumstances. Most important for the Realist plays, a central character wanted something, and the audience would watch as the character tried, scene by scene, to achieve his or her goal.

In the U.S., some of the earliest Realist plays were written and directed by David Belasco. Unlike his European counterparts, Belasco was writing melodramas, perhaps the most popular style of theatre in the U.S. during the 19th century (outside of minstrelsy and burlesque shows). When discussing the popularity of melodramas in the U.S., Daniel Gerould writes, "Crude, violent, dynamic in action, psychologically and morally simplistic, reliant on machinery and technological know-how for its powerful effects, melodrama became a direct expression of American society and national character" (7). Consider *Star Wars: Episode IV* as a modern-day melodrama: Luke Skywalker wears white, Darth Vader wears black, and Han Solo is a rogue who will be redeemed by the end of the story. This is not to say these plays were entirely unrealistic; that is, Belasco used this style in order to convey notions of the American character: who we are, and who we should attain to be as individuals and as a nation. What makes Belasco's Realism unique (and ornate) was his use of verisimilitude—that is, everything on stage had to look *exactly* as it does in life. Belasco used real money in his productions, rather than fake coins. Here is an extreme example: in order to create the sunset over the Sierra Nevada in his play, *The Girl of the Golden West* (1905), Belasco spent five thousand dollars over a period of three months to, as Belasco puts it, "secure exactly the soft colors of a Californian sunset" (Gerould, 24). Some of the failed sunsets were sold to other theatre companies. When remembering the effects used in *TGOTGW*, Belasco biographer William Winter states "[n]othing...I have ever seen in the Theatre has fully equaled in verisimilitude the blizzard on the Cloudy Mountain...such a bitter and cruel storm of wind-driven snow and ice as he had often suffered under in the strolling days of [Belasco's] nomadic youth" (206). Belasco's attention to detail, which some critics would say proved to be too much of a distraction on stage (Leiter, 6), caught the attention of Constantine

Stanislavski, creator of the "system," the basis for the American "method," which sought, above all, Truth in acting, directing, and writing.[1]

What is worth noting is that with any of these works—whether *A Doll House*, *Ms. Julie*, or *The Girl of the Golden West*—the story involves a central character who wants something, and we watch that character try to get what he or she wants. They live in a world that operates just outside their grasp and something incites them to change their world. The characters are psychologically driven to do what they do, and the plots are linear, cause-and-effect. Ultimately, the central character succeeds or fails, thereby supporting the writers' worldview.

There are some early American Realist writers who sought to break away from both verisimilitude and the simplistic entertainment values of melodrama in order to create a deeper realism. Members of the Provincetown Players in the 19-teens inspired what is known as The Little Theatre Movement. The Provincetown Players formed in 1915 under the direction of George Cook and his wife Susan Glaspell. They met in Provincetown, located on Cape Cod in Massachusetts. They were the first company to produce plays strictly written by American writers. Originally, they met in members' homes, but would later open The Provincetown Playhouse on MacDougal Street in Greenwich Village, downtown NYC. The Provincetown Players wished to capture the Bohemian feel of the West Bank: thought-inspired art, art-inspired thought. Susan Glaspell's *Trifles* is an early example of American Realism. In the play, a group of men investigate the home of a woman who is suspected of murdering her husband. Their wives are able to piece together the mystery: they learn, by examining the woman's broken jelly jars and finding the woman's dead bird, that the woman was in an abusive relationship and murdered her husband in order to escape constant physical and emotional violence. The play ends with the men being no closer to the answer, and the women keeping what they have discovered to themselves. As with Glaspell's other plays, this one is in opposition to the theories of Sigmund Freud, whose theories Glaspell and others found entirely sexist (with good reason, if you consider Freud's thoughts on passive female sexuality and penis envy). The audience should leave the play with the knowledge that women have a strong capacity for deductive reasoning, given their attention to detail—to what men may pass off as "trifles."

This overview of the origins of American Realism certainly overlooks a number of key players: Eugene O'Neill, another member of The Provincetown Players whose plays were produced on Broadway starting in 1920 (*Beyond the Horizon* and *The Emperor Jones*); Lillian Hellman (*The Children's Hour*, 1934), Clifford Odets, William Saroyan, and many others. Each one of these writers used Realism in his or her own fashion; however, each one also added something to the development of the American aesthetic. My reason for omitting them in this section is that they were bringing something else to their brand of Realism; in short, their Realism was an amalgam of European Realism as well as elements of the first-wave avant-garde, which sought to counter Realism as a dominant European aesthetic.

---

1 Ironically, The Group Theatre and later The Actors Studio had sought to calcify Stanislavski's psychological action/objective-based approaches as the standard of American acting and theatre creation, against the overtly ornate/melodramatic approaches to theatre used by Belasco and his contemporaries; yet, it was Belasco that Stanislavski made an honorary member of The Moscow Arts Theatre, given Belasco's desire to present "Truth" on stage (Marker, 178).

ALTERNATIVES TO REALISM

There have been a number of nonrealistic movements that have been better suited for the theatre than for any other medium. Symbolism, Expressionism, Futurism, Dadaism, Absurdism, Epic Theatre, Postdramatic Theatre, Language-Based Plays, Theatrical Jazz Aesthetic, and others have embraced theatricality—that is, writers and other artists affiliated with these styles fully invest in theatre's abstract nature, rather than presenting a surface representation of life. What follows is a very brief history of some of these movements or styles.

From the late 19th into the very early 20th centuries, artists believed that there was a capital-T "Truth" that could be discovered without the need for Dogma. Art could lead us to this Truth. For the Realists and Naturalists, Truth could be found with the presentation of life "as is;" however, artists affiliated with the first-wave avant-gardists disagreed, and each subset of the first wave had its own approach to finding the elusive Truth.

Broadly speaking, Symbolist writers were influenced by "Eastern" meditations. A number of exhibits from China and Japan had made their way across Europe, inspiring writers to consider action differently than writers of Realism. For the Realist, action was grounded in psychological cause-and-effect. For the Symbolist, the action was the "act" of quiet reflection; or, as Bert Cardullo and Robert Knopf suggest when talking of the work of Maurice Maeterlinck, the "action or conflict [was of] the internal kind, which enables us to penetrate deeper into the human consciousness" (43). In Maurice Maeterlinck's *Interior* (1894), a group of persons watch a family through a window and consider how they can tell the family that the daughter of the house has been found drowned. We watch the persons watch the family, until one finally enters the room; when the news is shared the mother opens up the backdoor and rushes out, farther away from the audience. The action is quite literally moving deeper and deeper on the stage. In other Symbolist works, the setting is not quite as realistic, and characters move among crystals and mirrors while questioning their own tormented soul. Examples include American poet Wallace Stevens' *Carlos Among the Candles* (1917) and French playwright and innovator Madame Rachilde's *The Crystal Spiders* (1892).

Expressionist playwrights questioned whether or not realism offered interrogations of the surface posing as depth, rather than presenting depth itself for consideration. According to Mel Gordon, "At the center of the Expressionist universe was Man. All other objects or conceptual phenomena—every physical property, theory, idea, formal grammar, science, or methodology—that precluded Man was eliminated or diminished" (16). The emphasis on man manifested in different Expressionist styles: The *Geist* Performance (in which the sound actors produced was emphasized over any other element), The *Schrei* Performance (in which actors "shifted from a kind of cataleptic stasis to a powerful, if epileptic, dynamism [...] against a backdrop distorted stage properties and painted backdrops"), and The *Ich* Performance, in which "the single ecstatic actor surrounded by or confronted with dozens of choral-performers who moved in unison, creating grotesque, but picturesque, poses") (18, 19, 20). Think of Expressionism like this: a central character has shrieked out his or her fractured soul on stage; each character, and even the set, is a manifestation of their fractured soul. Expressionism offered an allegory, empty of religious dogmatics, centering on a New Man, who had True self-awareness, but lacked political agency to change his world. He might have a name, but surrounding characters are allegorical, each being a fragment of his shouted soul that has been screamed out on stage. The sets would be nightmarish and angular, and the story could be confusing to follow—perhaps, somewhat nightmarish in its language and movement. The audience should leave contemplating the soul of man.

The Futurists differ from Expressionists insofar as one had to be a member of the Futurists in order to be considered a Futurist artist. Created by Filippo Tommaso Marinetti via the "Foundation and Manifesto of Futurism" in 1909, the Futurists were fascists (literally, as members were friends with Mussolini) who believed that all museums in Italy should be burned, paintings destroyed, and in its place the Gatling Gun, the motorcar, and any agent of speed and technology should be situated (Kirby, 3-9). The preferred theatre of the Futurist resembled the variety show (though the content was much more frenetic) (20). Their alogical short plays, called *synthesi*, were meant to disturb an audience, to anger them, to incite them into violence.

Dadaists, on the other hand, presented short, nonsensical works as a means of dismantling the myth of progress. Dadaism began with Hugo Ball, a German artist who moved to Switzerland during the First World War. Ball had been inspired by the work of Expressionist and Futurist artists; according to Mel Gordon, Ball had "dreamed of blending the emotionally heightened and self-centered world of Expressionism with the mechanical assuredness of Futurism" (Gordon *Dada Performance*, 11). However, after being on the front lines and witnessing the "faceless, body shattering thud of artillery fire and poison gas canisters," Ball rethought his theatre and the notion of progress (12). The myth of progress, Dadaists such as Hugo Ball argued, is what drove man to engage in the "faceless" "modern warfare" (12). Therefore, the Dadaists wanted no part of progress. Plays were rarely performed more than once, and were rarely rehearsed; after all, rehearsal leads to progress! The audience was supposed to be confused, delighted, charmed, and walk away with a different sense of self. As Mel Gordon suggests, "the Dadas shared Expressionism's sense of moral outrage and Futurism's aggressiveness, but only Dada produced a vision of absolute negativity, of complete and willful derision against a world destroying itself" (14). The audience was to be shaken to reconsider their role in the world and how the myth of progress could lead to violence in their personal lives.

There are a number of other styles that emerged in Europe during the early 20th century. Surrealist artists were inspired by Sigmund Freud's emphasis on the unconscious and used dream-imagery in their works. Antonin Artaud, a leading Surrealist writer, would later adapt Surrealism into what he called, Theatre of Cruelty: plays, he argued, should infect an audience like a plague; they should manifest in symptoms that the audience would carry with them out into the world. His theories were not quite put into practice until after his death, and those inspired by Artaud often find it necessary to temper his style (which includes constant shrieks and grunts from performers) with other approaches. Bertolt Brecht, meanwhile, developed his theories of Epic Theatre, built on a model by Erwin Piscator. Like Artaud, Brecht was a theorist, playwright, and director.

His theories, however, were much more concrete. He believed that performers should not delve into a character's emotions, but rather play their characters in quotation marks. The example he offers is "the street scene." Brecht correlates a theatre performance to an eye witness describing and enacting a car accident:

> The street demonstrator's performance is essentially repetitive. The event has taken place; what you are seeing now is a repeat. If the scene in the theatre follows the street scene in this respect, then the theatre will stop pretending not to be theatre, just as the street-corner demonstration admits it is a demonstration (and does not pretend to be the actual event). The element of rehearsal in the acting and of learning by heart in the text, the whole machinery and the whole process of preparation: it all becomes plainly apparent (122).

Brecht's theory that the theatre could "stop pretending not to be theatre" was foregrounded in the way he approached production. When directing his works, such as the 1928 musical *ThreePenny Opera* (written with Kurt Weill and Elisabeth Hauptmann), Brecht used title cards and announcers shouting the name of scenes in order to keep the audience from falling into empathy with the characters on stage. Brecht believed that empathy was lazy; rather, he wanted audience members to think above the play, to fully realize the play's Marxist agenda and to actively take that message into the world. The spectator was called upon to be an agent of social justice.

A number of American writers have used these avant-garde techniques in order to create a new *contract* with the audience. Eugene O'Neill is one example, as his plays *The Emperor Jones* and *Hairy Ape* are Expressionist: the first deals with colonialism, while the latter considers the separation of American classes.

Eugene O'Neill is often referenced as the starting point for serious American drama and his later works—such as *Long Day's Journey into Night* (1956) and *Moon for the Misbegotten* (1947)—are heralded as two of the most important plays of American Realism. However, in *The Other American Drama*, Marc Robinson argues that the entire canon of American drama needs to be reconsidered; rather than using O'Neill as a starting point for serious American dramatic literature, Gertrude Stein (a contemporary writer) should be "acknowledged as a major figure in American drama's adolescence" and "set alongside O'Neill in importance" (3). As a result, "an entire world of drama comes into clearer focus" (3). For Robinson, Stein's refusal to focus on "story," and her ability to make "time seem tangible, easily manipulated" as well as her "new dimensions of lyricism" "found in prosaic matters, like stage space and the human body," moves her away from the simple binary of "page and stage" and into a world of her own (3). With Stein, "Plays now looked sculpted, scored, or built, whereas before they seemed merely spilt onto page or stage" (3). Stein wanted the audience to be moved by their engagement with the theatre as a complete art-object, rather than watching a string of cause-and-effect lines of dialogue. Stein's avant-garde-theatre would inspire later Postdramatic auteurs, such as Robert Wilson, and Postmodern Theatre companies, such as The Wooster Group in NYC.

Sophie Treadwell is another American playwright who used avant-garde techniques in her writing. In *Machinal* (Broadway, 1928), Treadwell blends American Realism with Expressionism. The play is Realistic insofar as it was inspired by the true story of a named Ruth Snyder, who was executed for the murder of her husband. It is also a work of Realism because the audience needs to connect with Helen, the central character based on Snyder, who wishes for something more in her life, and that chance comes by way of an exciting young man who convinces her to kill her husband. Finally, and perhaps more important, it belongs under The Problem Play subheading of Realism as we are watching a woman who is told by society at large how she needs to behave, what she should want from her life, and most of all how she needs to abide without question, all of which leads to the act of murder and her execution. The play is a work of Expressionism insofar as the supporting characters are allegorical, lacking dimension; the world around her is a factory moving her from station-to-station, dictating how she needs to properly behave. When she meets the young man, she is awakened—a New Woman—but as with true Expressionism, she is powerless to fight against the world around her. She has political awareness, but not the agency to create change for herself. The machine rejects her as it were and she is put to death. The audience should be disturbed by this play, as it foregrounds the notion that for many women the only recourse to an unjust, male-dominated system is murder. The means of the message is quite harsh, but as with the works of Brecht, the audience is called upon to be a catalyst for social change and gender equality.

A number of other playwrights have also successfully created works that allow for some abstraction, some dream-like space. For example, the original title of Arthur Miller's *Death of a Salesman* (1949) was *The Inside of His Head*, as Miller had hoped to create a work of American Expressionism—consider the moments where Willy is remembering his past: these moments are created by Willy's mind. What is he leaving out, what is he celebrating, and what is he trying to forget (Robinson, *The American Play*)? Consider Tennessee Williams' *The Glass Menagerie*: Williams had hoped to incorporate both Brecht's use of projections, as well as a poetic language using crystals as a metaphor (crystal, glass, and mirrors were all favorite metaphors for Symbolist writers) into Realist works in order to create what he called a "plastic theatre" (Williams *Production Notes*, 24). Unfortunately, the projections suggested in *The Glass Menagerie* are almost never used in production, as they provide too much of a distraction to the world of story on stage. A label often applied to Tennessee Williams is "Poetic Realism," given his love for language, his long passages of dialogue, and the dream-like world of story Williams is able to create through his haunted characters and settings.

As American and European theatre continued in the post-war era, other "isms" emerged. Historian Martin Esslin applies the label "theatre of the absurd" to the early postwar dramas. Looking at European writers such as Samuel Beckett and Eugene Ionesco, Esslin argues, "Theatre of the Absurd shows the world as an incomprehensible place. The spectators see the happenings on the stage entirely from the outside, without ever understanding the full meaning of these strange patterns of events as newly arrived visitors might watch life in a country of which they have not mastered the language" (14). American examples include Edward Albee's *Zoo Story*, which beings innocently enough with a man sitting on a park bench (a Sunday habit) and another man approaching him to tell him about a visit to the zoo. They take twists and turns in their conversation exploring themes of loneliness, isolation, and miscommunication until one man ends up accidentally aiding the other in a gruesome suicide.

The absurdist dramas are the bridge between Modernism (the era of capital-T Truth), and Postmodernism (not capital-T truth, though there may be performative, individual "truths"). Postmodernism simply means "after Modernism." In a sense, Postmodern works build on (or play with) past ways of telling the story in order to problematize present-day assumptions. Postmodernism evolved post World War II. If Dada was the result of faceless warfare, the Postmodern condition came about after Auschwitz and the dropping of the bombs on Hiroshima and Nagasaki. Progress lead to the extermination of thousands, on one hand by the death clerks who treated genocide as a banal activity in Nazi Germany, and the atomic bomb that could massacre thousands upon thousands of people. The events following World War II would lead to the Cold War, in which the Communist Bloc and the Western Capitalist World lived in a state of mutually-assured destruction. For the Postmodern philosopher, it is the myth of progress, the myth of Truth, which continues to create the conditions for war, for colonization, for diminishing and destroying the human Other.

By the 1960s, the wish to create ethical relationships with the Other guided a number of art movements, including the folk and spoken-word scene in Greenwich Village. The Off-Off Broadway theatre was born in this context. A number of plays written for smaller venues, such as the Caffe Cino, dealt with gay and lesbian identity, dissatisfaction with the heteronormative world, and foregrounded the broken myths of America. A number of important writers emerged from the Off-Off Broadway movement, including Robert Patrick, Doric Wilson, Lanford Wilson, Sam Shepard, Maria Irene Fornes, and Jack Gelber. Some of the plays were Realistic and others offered play-within-a-play scenarios. For example, in Jack Gelber's *The Connection* (1959), the actors portrayed homeless men and women who were performing a play in which they showed the audience what it looks like to wait for heroin. A live band was also on stage playing jazz throughout the evening. We can consider this kind of theatre "total theatre;" that is, the theatre becomes a multi-faceted jewel that draws the audience in and submerges them in the complete world of story. Are the actors in the play actually homeless people? Is the story being told true?

The 1970s and '80s saw the emergence of the language-based playwrights. In *New Playwriting Strategies*, Paul Castagno offers a vocabulary for the language-based playwrights and how their "new poetics" has been fused with traditional forms in order to create a new theatre aesthetic (for the late 20th and early 21st centuries). Castagno successfully argues that the language-based-playwright is a *hybrid* writer, "marking contemporary playwrights' unease with traditional narrative through a conflation of dramaturgies and source materials" (5). Language-based-plays rely on "metatheatrics" but also rely on traditional narrative forms as a "lifeline" for audiences (5). What Castagno is suggesting is that early 21st century writers are diving into more abstract territory by playing with an audience's cultural awareness and memory.

One example of a language-based-playwright is Neal Bell, whose plays include *Two Small Bodies* (1977), *On the Bum* (1992), and *Monster* (2002, an adaptation of Mary Shelley's *Frankenstein)*. When discussing the work of Neal Bell, theorist Frederic Jameson writes:

> In Neal Bell's plays, the dramatic situation is not particularly one in which something dramatic happens, but rather in which people begin to reinvent their replies to one another; not one in which something significant gets said, let alone expressed, but rather one in which that peculiar business of talking to someone else begins to take place—to take place again, one might be tempted to say, if any memory remained of the earlier times (Jameson, 372).

In other words, Bell's play relies on the modern convention of dialogue, but unlike the Realistic drama, Bell's text is empty of the notion of dialogue as the means of creating cause-and-effect action. Rather, Bell's drama is part of a theatrical movement that "allows the new [language-based] theater to develop its mysterious connections with the very roots and sources of language itself, in conversation" (372). In short, we are watching characters trying to create empathy via feeble attempts at communication, in stark contrast to the convention of driving a plot via dialogue.

Other language-based-playwrights include Sam Shepard, Maria Irene Fornes, and Charles Mee. Language-based-playwrights rely on known works or archetypes in order to make familiar tropes *unfamiliar* to audiences; with these works, philosophical questions are foregrounded over a tight, linear narrative. Len Jenkin's *Dark Ride*, for example, begins with a quest for a precious stone. However, the various characters talk to the audience throughout the play in an effort to divert focus. When all of the characters meet on stage at the end, they continue to expound their views on the world to the audience, to anyone who will listen. One by one, characters react, stating, "I'm not interested in philosophy. Just tell me how it ends" (45-46). Are the characters suggesting they understand the audience's paranoia—that there simply is no ending to the story? Or, is it perhaps a question about life itself, and how will each of us meet our end? Charles Mee invites directors to add to his play *Under Construction*, which offers a view of the U.S.A. from the 1950s to the present day. Gender roles are questioned, national identity is interrogated, and actors are free to engage with the audience, to create new movement, add monologues, poetry, anything which can highlight concerns, questions, and emotions that come with living in a country that often enforces binaries based on how one is supposed to behave. With language-based-plays, audiences are left asking questions, specifically to how we try to construct meaning for our existence when there is no capital-T "Truth."

In lower Manhattan, the early 21st century saw the beginning of Geek Theatre. Like the language-based-plays, Geek Theatre plays with an audience's cultural memory. Unlike language-based-plays, the cultural memory is specific to fans of comic books, video games, anime, and Sci-Fi Fantasy (what literary theorists refer to as "the genres") (Bray *Geek Theatre*). For example, Crystal Skillman's *Geek!*, produced by the Vampire Cowboys in 2013, is a mash-up (or, to use Castagno's term, a hybrid; I prefer "mash-up" for its immediacy and relevancy to younger writers) of Dante's Inferno and Anime convention. The key character is searching the Con, which is about to close in seconds, in order to meet her hero, an anime artist. Geek Theatre embraces its audiences as fans, and as a result, Geek plays have become popular in theatres across the U.S. A visible example would be Qui Nguyen's *She Kills Monsters*, which has enjoyed Off Broadway, regional, and independent/community theatre productions.

There are two more current aesthetic movements worth mentioning: the first is postdramatic theatre. In his book, *Postdramatic Theatre*, Hans-Thies Lehmann looks at the rise of theatre *auteurs* who reduce the primacy of the playtext in order to create a theatre-as-aesthetic-experience. For example, director Robert Wilson (not a playwright in the traditional sense, but nevertheless, a primary artist) begins by sketching set designs. His collaborators are then asked to create music and movement around the set. Such was the case with *Einstein on the Beach* (1976), Wilson's most popular work, which was written with composer Philip Glass, and featured a libretto co-authored by Christopher Knowles, Lucinda Childs, and Samuel M. Johnson. Wilson plays with time, space, and sound. He invites his audience to appreciate the images and movement, to meditate, to zone out.

Theatrical jazz aesthetic is another late 20th century innovation. According to Joni L. Jones and Iya Omi Osun Olomo, the theatrical jazz aesthetic dates back to "the Black Arts Movement in the Sounds in Motion Harlem dance studio under the tutelage of Dianne McIntyre" (598). As Jones and Olomo suggest:

> A theatrical jazz aesthetic borrows many elements from the musical world of jazz—improvisation, process over product, ensemble synthesis, solo virtuosity— and disrupts the traditional conventions of Western theatre [...] A theatrical jazz aesthetic uses gestural language as counterpoint to the verbal text. This gestural language is a blend of modern dance, contemporary dance, popular idioms, and everyday physical references. [...] Productions are as much about painting the space with bodies as they are about filling the air with words. The bodies have their own stories to tell, and the performers' visceral negotiations between their physical selves and the physical realities of the various characters enacted becomes a vital component of the experience. [...] Like a fine jazz ensemble, theatrical jazz relies on the confident collaboration of artists who have come to trust each other, and to trust their own creative impulses through long term repeated partnerships (599-600).

An example of a play using the theatrical jazz aesthetic is *For Colored Girls Who Have Considered Suicide When the Rainbow Is Enuf* by playwright/poet Ntozake Shange. The play embraces the stage as a true, abstract space. Seven women engage with the audience—their words are lyrical, playful, dangerous, and grounded in a truth that transcends the Realistic, cause-and-effect story structure, but nevertheless *feels Real*. The play, which the author suggests is a *choreopoem*, offers exciting possibilities to writers who wish to blend poetic arts, drama, movement, and music. The audience should feel as if the piece not only addresses them, their needs, their desires, but embraces them, challenges them, welcomes them, dances with them.

Some of the techniques of the theatrical jazz aesthetic have been blended with other styles of drama. For example, in *Topdog/Underdog*, Suzan-Lori Parks captures the sound of jazz in the rhythm of the characters' dialogue; the play itself is more-or-less realistic, as it deals with two brothers—a con-man and a reformed con who is trying to make a living. The con-man, Booth, wants his brother to get back into the game and to teach him how to win at Three-Card-Monte. Lincoln, however, is off the grift, or at least appears to be, until the play's devastating conclusion. The play is also language-based, as the characters are named "Booth" and "Lincoln," and Lincoln himself dresses as Honest Abe, complete with whiteface, for a job he has at a Coney-Islandesque amusement park. Night after night he dresses up and audiences pay to pretend they are assassinating him. The audience is left to contemplate the nature of family of history and cultural memory (which are often at odds with one another), as well as the nature of brotherhood. It is a compelling piece.

What I wish to stress is that writers in each of these forms are trying to incite the audience to do something (engage with self, engage in war, engage in peace), or to be something (as in Melodrama's presentation of the myth of the American character). The playwrights' focus is always on the audience; at the same time, you, the playwright, should be familiar with these other paths taken up by fellow writers. Read plays. Read every play you can lay your hands on, and never stop reading.

INTERNAL LOGIC AND CONTRACT WITH THE AUDIENCE

This look back at the dominant aesthetics of the 20th and 21st centuries should help us understand that even if a work is not Realistic, it still obeys by a set of aesthetic principles. Let us call this the play's *contract with the audience*. Early in the play, the audience should know what style of work they are watching, as well as which character (in cases of more realistic works) they are supposed to follow and/or root for. For example, playwright Marsha Norman suggests that by page eight, audience members want to know "what is at stake?" (Norman). She also suggests that "the audience wants to know what it's waiting for, why are you telling this story, what do you want from them?" (Norman). For Norman, the audience is "like a jury, they need to know what the person is accused of so they can know how to listen to the information, render a judgment, and be dismissed" (Norman). Her suggestions, of course, work tremendously well for Realistic plays. However, we should not dismiss them even if a work is non-realist. The audience still needs to understand fairly early on what journey they are going to take—even if (especially if) the journey has more to do with aesthetics (postdramatic works, postmodern and/or deconstructivist works) rather than psychologically-driven action; the audience needs an "in," and needs to be able to follow.

You as the writer need to create the world of story, which includes an aesthetic language as well as an *internal logic*, or consistency. Dialogue can help create the internal logic of the piece. Consider David Rabe's *Hurlyburly*. At first blush, the play comes off the page as incredibly realistic: a group of men working in Hollywood deal with the crumbling façade of performed masculinity. However, their word choices (their language) is not entirely realistic—their use of "rapeteta" and "blah, blah, blah" is not necessarily part of everyday speech. However, most of the characters in the play use these phrases at different points in the play. The language creates an internal logic: because everyone in this world of story does this (that is, because of the consistency), it becomes accepted. If one of the characters were to ask, "how come you all are talking like this?" the logic would be broken. It is simply accepted.

HOW CAN WE DEFINE THE AMERICAN PLAYWRIGHT?

In the playwriting world, there is a very divisive argument about whether playwriting is a craft or an art, and whether a playwright should be considered a craftsperson or an artist. One of the agreed-upon factors in the argument is that a *craft* is something that can be learned, whereas an *art* is not. Jeffrey Sweet begins *The Dramatists' Toolkit: The Craft of the Working Playwright* by stating, "I have strong ideas about what kinds of people are most likely to become real working playwrights: actors and journalists. Not novelists" (1). For Sweet, the playscript is not literature (an art), and those who write with a literary bent tend not to consider how well something might *play* on stage, rather, they will focus on how it reads on a page (1). Sweet views playwriting as a craft which can be learned by deeply understanding the actor's vocabulary and/or the journalist's ability to tell (and edit) a cause-and-effect story. The successful application of the actor's or journalist's skills in playwriting is a craft.

Nigerian-born playwright Femi Euba, on the other hand, suggests that the playwright may be viewed as a kind of ritual quester. In his book, *Poetics of the Creative Process*, Euba focuses on the Yoruba religion, and considers ritual as a three-step process involving need, sacrifice, and efficacy. Euba described his book as "meditations on playwriting" (personal conversation). Although Euba's definition of the playwright as ritual-quester falls outside of the immediate craft vs. art debate, I do find his "meditations" to be gorgeous. What I would like to hold onto for this book is the notion of the playwright as a person who is thoughtful and responsible for/to his or her immediate community. Even if a work becomes hailed by critics as "universal," it should be in a playwrights' interest to write for a specific, local community.

I have already talked at length about the language-based playwright. What is key for Castagno's definition is that the playwright is a collage-maker. Castagno sees playwriting as an art rather than a craft. For our purposes, I want you to consider both impulses: that is, the content of the piece is what makes your work an art and you an artist. The form the piece needs to be crafted in order for you to adhere to your contract with the audience. The impulse that incited you to write is akin to that of a ritual-quester, and the thought you wish to communicate to your community is something that needs to be deeply felt and deeply meditated by both writer and audience.

An example of a playwright I would consider both a craftsperson and an artist is August Wilson. Wilson's works incorporate elements of cause-and-effect and psychological realism, while also meditating on shared cultural memories in the African American Community.[2] Wilson breaks the standard cause-and-effect structure of psychological realism (in which any sequence that does not propel the story forward is cut) by allowing digressions in the form of character monologues. We learn more about what makes a character "tick" in these moments, even though the action of the play takes a brief pause. For Wilson, these digressions also serve to remind the audience of the context of the play—the human history, and all that has been lost in the African American communities due to gentrification and notions of progress.[3] It is in these moments the audience is given the opportunity to truly care for a character and to better grasp the complicated, underlying themes of any of Wilson's work.

While there are tomes written about how a playwright writes (a solitary figure over mounds of paper, everything stained with coffee rings to a key collaborator working with directors, actors, dramaturgs, etc.), the bottom line is a playwright is in cultural conversation with their immediate region. Playwrights write their own letter to the world, which is shaped in development and rehearsal, and is received by the public. From there, the public takes the play out into the world to consider its message, its aesthetic, and to ultimately decide if the experience —the night at the theatre—was worth their time. We as writers hate this last part, but it is perhaps the most important aspect of any theatrical performance. Did we engage with the audience in such a way that they never doubt their time was well spent, even if (especially if) they did not care for the show? I have seen many "beautiful failures," and while I could not in earnest recommend the plays, I was certainly glad I went. I would much prefer these plays to the safe, sure bets that get a lot of attention at regional and commercial theatres. The tightrope you will learn to walk is allowing the audience to feel a sense of danger without turning them off entirely. Your audience must be engaged.

CONCLUSION

The playwright is the great instigator. The title of this book is a play on the old dramatic writing structure (exposition, inciting incident, rising action, climax, and denouement). So much has been written about that form already (from conflations of Aristotle and Horace, to Scribe and Freytag, to most screenwriting books), that we tend to overlook that most important word "incite." When we write, we are trying to incite action in an audience: an audience needs to be moved, and furthermore, moved to do something. At the same time, this book

2 For an excellent discussion on how late 20th-century playwrights used realism to question the naturalist/rationalist ways of seeing, read William Demastes' Beyond Naturalism: A New Realism in American Theatre, New York: Greenwoord Press, 1988.
3 For a longer discussion, see playwright Suzan-Lori Parks' interview with August Wilson in the November 2005 issue of *American Theatre* magazine.

is meant to empower young writers by helping you create strategies to not only write a script, but to see it through development and production by creating your own opportunities. It is one heck of a journey and it is my goal to see you through.

QUESTIONS:

1. Consider your favorite play. What is the piece's internal logic? What is the play's contract with the audience? What does this play borrow from the past (in terms of aesthetics)? How does the play speak to a 21st century audience? More importantly, what does the play communicate to you? Why does it resonate with you? Spend some time with these questions and jot your thoughts on the following page. This is not a formal essay assignment—this is just meant for you.

2. Have you ever seen a play or movie that broke its contract with the audience? How did this make you feel? What did you think was going to happen? In what ways were you disappointed? In what ways were you surprised?

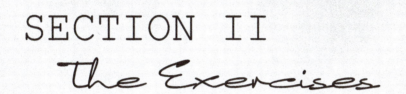

SECTION II
The Exercises

CHAPTER *one*

OBJECTS

In most dramatic writing classes and books on dramatic writing, young writers are asked to create a scene having to do with objects.[1] During my first semester as a graduate student, my instructor, Jim Ryan, asked us to look through magazines (mostly photography magazines with portraits; some were studio, some were out in the world), and find a face that resonated with us. We were then asked to free-write for a while from the perspective of the person we had chosen. Who was this person? What did this person want? Just let the person talk freely. Let the person find his or her voice.

From there, we were asked to look through antique catalogues and find an object. I picked out an original National-O resonator guitar. We were asked to have the character we had created based on the photo talk about the object and its importance. Why does that person want the object or possess it? What would happen if they gained the object, or lost it? This became the first fully realized character I ever created. I had written short plays in college, but this was truly the first time it all made sense to me. I created a character, who I now

---

1 See Jeffrey Sweet's chapter, "Negotiating Over Objects" in *The Dramatists' Toolkit*.

call Mr. Coffee, and his guitar was the most important thing in the world to him. The resulting play, *Goodnight Lovin' Trail*, about a man who misplaces his guitar, has been in rep. with the Rising Sun Performance Company Off-Off Broadway for over ten years. Why has the play had some lasting quality? What is it about objects? What can we learn about our possessions or how we interact with them?

Let's imagine this scenario for a moment: a young man and a young woman (or another young man) have been involved with each other for several weeks. They have not labeled their situation. Perhaps if anyone were to ask, the term "casual" could be applied. But one morning, after a "casual" evening, the young man wakes up on his own (perhaps his casual acquaintance needed to go to work, etc.), and he goes to his sink. He reaches for his toothbrush. He makes a discovery. A second toothbrush, relatively new, is in the rinse cup right next to his toothbrush. What is the casual acquaintance trying to tell the young man?

We in the audience have an immediate response to this. We can recognize the panic that can come with an object as heavily coded as a toothbrush. Now, the young man has to do something. If he picks it up, smiles, and dances around the room singing, "You're a Pink Toothbrush, I'm a Blue Toothbrush," what can we discern about the young man? Is he ready for a status upgrade?

Now, another scenario: imagine that the young man sees the toothbrush; his jaw drops, his eyes widen. He looks around. He carries the toothbrush as if to ask for something…an explanation…anything…but, oh, yeah, the other person isn't there. He goes back into the bathroom, looks at the mirror, looks at the toothbrush; closing his eyes, he extends his arm over the wastebasket and releases the toothbrush. It hits the bottom of the basket. He opens his eyes, looks in the mirror. Pale white. He turns. His expression softens. He looks back into the wastebasket, carefully picks up the toothbrush. Smiles at it. He gives it a rinse. He puts it back in, next to his own. He keeps looking at the new toothbrush next to his. It happens again—PANIC! He picks it up and drops it in the wastebasket. He turns away and runs out of the room. He re-enters the room, eyes wide, and stares at the wastebasket. What can we discern about this young man? How does he feel?

A third example: a young man sees the new toothbrush. He scoffs at it. He picks it up. He figures these tiles on the floor needs cleaning, the toilet could use a detailed scrubbing, the shower head, everything. He makes a mess out of the toothbrush. He puts it back in the cup and texts his casual acquaintance, "come on over and brush your teeth." What can we discern about this young man (aside from the possibility that he was created by Neil Labute)?

The first young man clearly loves the idea of being in a relationship with casual acquaintance. It is what he has waited for. He might be a bit over the top in his enthusiasm, which might not make him the most relatable to a large audience, though some of us have had the joy (or at least, imagined the joy) of feeling accepted by another person.

The third young man is a jerk. Pure and simple. An audience will not like him at all, unless we are given a very clear reason why he would behave in such a way. And it has to be something that would make us hate the casual acquaintance, but accept that young man would still sleep with him/her. This is very complicated and too much to pack into a single beat. Chances are, he's just a jerk, and we hate him. Justifiably.

The second young man shows the most conflict. On one hand, we see that he could accept this new person as a hashtag-significant other. However, there are pressures holding him back. We're not sure what they are and we probably don't need to right now. Moving a relationship forward, regardless of the circumstances, can be terribly unnerving; this alone makes the second young man the most relatable (and we do hope, if he accepts the new status, he'll buy a new toothbrush before bringing casual acquaintance back over).

I give this lengthy example as a way of highlighting how we imbue *stuff*. In a play, a toothbrush is never just a toothbrush. Nor should it be! In life, we have favorite objects, and we imbue them as our own. Consider this example: my son had a small Batman toy. It was his favorite thing in the entire world. He lost it one day when we were out. Backtracking was not a possibility, as we had run too many errands. I went ahead and bought him a new Batman toy, the *exact same toy*. However, it was not the same. It wasn't his. Two weeks later, he found the Batman toy. It was stuck somewhere in the car (and I swear, I searched everywhere. I have no idea what vortex exists in the vehicle that can devour, and spit back, Batman toys). The first thing he did was have the old Batman beat up the new Batman. Why was he so upset about the lost toy? Because it was his! The new one was not his, it was an imposter, and deserved the beating with Batman's "hammers of justice."

Exercise One:

Begin by taking out several books of black-and-white photos of random persons from your library. I suggest finding books featuring the photos of Diane Arbus, Robert Maplethorpe, or Robert Frank. There are so many to choose from. Make sure you give yourself a wide number of choices.

Part I
1. Find a photograph of a person in one of these books. You will be spending time with this person.
    a. After you find a picture: study it. Spend some time with that person.
    b. What is that person saying to you right this second? (If they only say one thing, like, "hey, buddy, got a light?" or "what are you staring at?"—try to find a way to keep the conversation going.) Discover this character's rhythms of speech and his or her worldview.
2. Find a photograph of an object from one of the antique books.
    a. Write down every detail about the object. What it looks like, what you imagine its weight to be, if there's a description of how old the object is, why it resonates with you personally, etc.

Part II
1. Take the character you have created, and allow him or her to talk about the object you studied as if it were one of his or her most valuable possessions. As the character talks, continue to discover his or her rhythm of speech and his or her or worldview. Take your time.

Part III

1. Your character enters a room. There is another character in there.* Now, you have two options:
   a. Your character wants said object. It has gone missing? Maybe someone is trying to sell it? Maybe someone has stolen it? Your character wants that object back. Does the second character have it?
   b. Your character wants to get rid of the object and is having trouble unloading it on the second character.

*If you are having trouble creating a second character, go back to the books of photos and find someone new. Perform Part I with this new person. Bring this person together with the first person you created and proceed to Parts II and III.

Exercise Two

Take this…

One of the first exercises I learned while a graduate student in Neal Bell's advanced playwriting classes is "This is my past," based on a scene in *Anatol*, a play by Austrian playwright Arthur Schnitzler about a playboy and his romantic exploits and woes. In a scene entitled "Episode," Anatol brings his friend Max a box of letters from his past, hoping that Max will take them as he plans to head to the countryside and start his life anew. The exercise by Bell based on this scene remains one of my all-time favorites (so much so that I joke with students that I want my epitaph to read "This is my past…"). Though the exercise belongs to Mr. Bell (to whom I am deeply indebted), over the past ten years I have adapted it to meet the needs of my introductory class.

1. Have character A approach character B with an object. Character A says, "take this." Character B says, "why." Character A discusses what the object is and why Character B needs to take it. The scene goes on for however long the scene goes on.
2. Character A approaches Character B with something that belongs to Character B, and says, "Take this back!" Character B presents an obstacle: "I cannot!" Continue the scene between the two characters, being sure to name the object in the dialogue, and the reason why A can no longer have it and B cannot take it back.

CONCLUSION

These exercises should help you with a number of goals for your scene and for your play. First, human beings are inherently dramatic. When you started Exercise Two, and Character A said to Character B "Take this," did Character B respond with "Thank you," thereby ending the scene? Or did Character B ask "why?" The second we ask "why" in a scene, we have created dramatic tension. (And when you have Character B ask "why," or create some other kind of block, you are proving my point about human beings. Only once in ten years of teaching these exercises has someone chosen to simply have Character B say, "thank you," and she later confessed that she did it to knock me off my high horse!) Dramatic tension can be subtle, but it always must be present in some way. For example, in Maurice Maeterlinck's *Interior*, two characters (The Old Man and Stranger) argue over the best way to present the news to a family their daughter has drowned. In this piece, the characters are more philosophical and reflexive than characters featured in works of Realism (that is, we are not fed the "in a world, one man" narrative). Nevertheless, the scene still relies on dramatic tension. Perhaps the best explanation for the necessity of dramatic tension comes from Robert Ball's excellent *Backwards and Forwards*, in which he states, "Dramatic tension requires that the audience desire to find out what is coming up. The greater the desire, the greater—and more active—the audience's involvement" (59). Keep in mind, at some point in our writing, we need to consider what we are trying to incite our audience to feel, think, and finally, do.

Second, having the characters discuss an object can help us get around exposition (a point made by Jeffrey Sweet). When we talk about objects we hold dear, we are telling others what our interests are and how we view the world and ourselves in the world via the things we value. There is an area of study known as "thing theory," which, broadly speaking, suggest we can learn just as much about mankind by what we make, what physical objects we hold close, and what objects we desire, as we can from studying evolutionary theory (some theorists wisely suggest studying the two together, rather than setting up yet another humanities vs. science debate).[2] Consider Laura's unicorn in *The Glass Menagerie*. The unicorn is how she sees herself: different, fragile. When Jim breaks her out of her shell—and simultaneously, breaks the horn off the glass unicorn—she tells him, "It's no tragedy, Freckles. Glass breaks so easily (....) I'll just imagine he had an operation. The horn was removed to make him feel less freakish. Now he will feel more at home with the other horses, the ones that don't have horns" (125). Laura, who has been shy to the point of sickness, now calls Jim "Freckles," a very bold step. Furthermore, the way she discusses the unicorn is really what she is telling Jim he has done for her. Williams is a bit heavy-handed with this scene, granted.

In the Next Room (or, The Vibrator Play) (2009), playwright Sarah Ruhl dramatizes the early, medicinal uses of the vibratory, which was said to relieve "hysteria" by bringing women to orgasm. Over the course of the play, the cold, detached doctor who attempts to teach his female patients the scientific reasons (meaning, late 19th century science, loaded with "mansplaining") why their bodies react as they do, and why the treatment is important. Ultimately, the doctor's wife will use a number of tactics as she teaches her husband how to be her lover. In the end, the vibrator represents detachment from sex, while the human bodies represent all of the messy and wonderful desires that lead to sexual fulfillment.

In *Star Wars*, Ben Kenobi offers Luke Skywalker his father Anakin Skywalker's lightsaber, giving Kenobi the opportunity to discuss the Jedi and the Force. This lets the audience know more about the world of the story and the journey

---

2 For a comprehensive look at thing theory, please read Bill Brown's "Thing Theory" in *Critical Inquiry*, Volume 28 no. 1. Also look at Peter Miller's essay, "How Objects Speak," that appears in *The Chronicle of Higher Education* (http://chronicle.com/article/How-Objects-Speak/148177/?cid=cr&utm_source=cr&utm_medium=en).

Luke will have to take in order to become a Jedi Master. A final example: the pocket-watch in *Pulp Fiction*. We learn that it is a very important watch for Butch, a boxer who has decided not to throw a fight by killing the other boxer in the ring, and who will go back to his apartment despite the danger. (I suggest you go ahead and watch the movie to find out for yourself why the watch is so important.)

As you move forward with your writing, consider what objects your characters hold near-and-dear and why. This will help you move around exposition, give the audience a view into the world of story, and create compelling dramatic tension.

CHAPTER *two*

GETTING THE ACTION INTO THE BODY/CREATING ACTIVE SCENES

When I was a kid, I had a terrible time keeping my emotions "in." On more than one occasion, I remember my mother saying to me, "never play poker." Has this ever happened to you? Have you behaved in a way that tipped people off to what you might be thinking or feeling, even if (*especially* if) you did not want others to know what was actually going on inside of you? What you were doing was performing an aspect of yourself, or to put it in performance studies terms, "performing the self."

The field of performance studies has complicated our view of the act of performance. For the scholar and student of performance studies, the term *performance* means "restored behavior." Restored behavior, or "twice-behaved behavior," has been explained as the "Physical or verbal actions that are not-for-the-first time, prepared, or rehearsed. A person may not be aware that she is performing a strip of restored behavior" (*Performance Studies*, 29). So, when your inner life manifests in some kind of gesture, no matter how subtle, and it is something that you are unaware of, you are engaging in a restored behavior.

In the theatre, the audience watches actors *perform*, which in theatre studies, refers to the act of pretending to be another person (or animal, or object) relying on the mutual imaginations of the performer and the audience for the performance. The performance may include written dialogue and bodily behaviors as a means of engaging with other performers and the audience. For playwrights, it is our job not only to create dialogue, but to suggest behaviors (in dialogue, stage directions, or via subtext) that can be "read" by an audience. This is one of the reasons why a number of early plays read more like novels, and why so much early dialogue is on the nose: we forget we are watching people *do*.

Furthermore, we need to understand that in most plays (whether Realistic or not), characters have *objectives*, which simply means that they want something from the other characters in the play. The objectives can be simple ("I want you to listen to me"), they can be complex ("I am owed a measure of respect from the world; therefore, I am going to make you respect me"), but somehow the objectives have to tune us into the character's larger wants, and their larger philosophies. In most cases, the objectives are not plainly stated. Rather, the characters behave a certain way that suggests their wants, and the audience will interpret both the words and the bodily behavior in order to have a grounded understanding of the character. In other words, we are watching the characters *do* because there is something they *want*.

The exercise in this chapter will focus on getting the words "into the body." The writer will be forced to move around in a space in order to fully understand that drama is "to do." We will take some time to consider what the body does in the space and how a body can be read as a text. We will also consider the notion of subtext and when a word should not be spoken.

One of my favorite books on the technique of acting is Robert Cohen's *Acting One*. He offers a number of what he calls "contentless scenes," in which actors are given easy to memorize lines (for example, two acting partners may say sequential numbers back and forth at each other) and a condition (for example, one actor may be told that she believes that her acting partner means to murder her, while the partner has been told that she believes she has just found her long-lost sister) (Cohen, 39-44). I believe the contentless scene should be considered by writers in order to fully understand how the body communicates even more so than the words. The words can only communicate so much. If someone tells you, "Oh, I just love ham!" and picks up a piece of ham and eats it, smiling, we know it to be true. If someone tells you, "Oh, I just love ham!" winces, and tosses the ham in the trash, we know they are being sarcastic.

EXERCISE THREE: ONE WORD AT A TIME

In this exercise, I want you and a partner (someone in class or someone you might live with or hang out with, etc.) to perform a scene in which each of you will only be allowed to say one word at a time. The first person wants to leave the room. The second person wants the first person to stay. Perform the exercise twice, playing each role. It might look like this:

```
(CHARACTER A heads for the door)
```

```
CHARACTER B
(Blocking the door)
Wait!

CHARACTER A
Can't.

CHARACTER B
Please.

CHARACTER A
Bye.

CHARACTER B
Cookies!

CHARACTER A
(Stops)
Cookies?

CHARACTER B
Hot.

CHARACTER A
Can't.

CHARACTER B
Can't?

CHARACTER A
Can't!!!!
```

From here Character A will leave. Sometimes, writers find a way to keep Character A in the room. Sometimes, while improvising, the one playing Character B will block the door. The key to this exercise is to get the words in your body. Our writing is action-based. People are doing something to affect each other.

Once you have completed this game playing both Character A and Character B, I want you to write a short scene (2-3 properly formatted pages) in which Character A wants something, and Character B blocks Character A from his or her goal. It can be as simple as leaving the room. It could be that Character A wants to finish the last of the coffee. *Keep it simple*.

TACTICS AND PERSPECTIVES

Just as in life, if characters want something, they have to find a way to get what they want. They have to make the other person *feel* something that compels them to comply. As stated by Robert Cohen, "Tactics are the strategies of human communication; they are the active ingredients of dynamic interactions" (34). Characters have to employ strategies in order to achieve their objectives in the scene. So, if we define *objective* as the question, "what do I want?" from the character's point of view, tactics would be the question, "what do I have to do to get what I want?" We want our characters to influence each other's point of view.

Drama educator Dorothy Heathcote uses the term *perspectives*, which is agreeable in this circumstance. In his book *Transforming Teaching and Learning with Active and Dramatic Approaches*, Brian Edmiston foregrounds the notion of drama educator Dorothy Heathcote's "perspectives," built on Erving Goffman's concept of framing an event. Edmiston quotes Heathcote at length, which is worth repeating here:

> In any social encounter, there are two aspects present. One is the *action* necessary for the event to progress forward toward conclusion. The other is the *perspective* from which people are coming to enter the event. This is frame, and frame is the main agent in providing tension and meaning for the participants" (Edmiston's emphasis, 204).

While the above passage is taken from a longer conversation about working with grammar students to help them articulate their individual perspectives on "real-and-imagined events," I do feel that it is useful for the writer to use in a prescriptive way. Each character comes with his or her own highly personal point of view (perspective), and the forward action occurs as the two characters come to an understanding via how they make each other feel. The result may be that an objective is fulfilled; it could be that a character had an objective, but then had a change of heart; either way, your characters need to listen and you as a writer should understand how your characters *effect/affect* each other.

EXERCISE FOUR: FOLLOW ME

With this exercise, writers will be asked to work with others (in groups of three) in order to experience a choice between two people, in order to understand how to make others feel compelled *to do*. One participant will face the other two participants in a triangular formation. Person A, the one facing the other two, will have to make a choice: do I follow the person on my left or the person on my right? The person on the right will offer the phrase, "follow me." Person A will repeat the phrase, "follow me," as it was stated by the person on the right (including any gestures). The person on the left will then say, "follow me," and Person A will repeat the phrase including any gestures. This will continue, back and forth, until Person A feels compelled to follow one or the other. Make sure that each one in the group has the opportunity to be both Person A and the one with the objective.

After you have performed this exercise, ask yourself:

As Person A, what made me feel compelled to follow one person and not the other? What tactics worked on me? As the character with the objective, what tactics did I use in order to influence Person A's decision? What worked? What didn't work? How were my tactics perceived by Person A? How did I make them feel? (Consider that making someone *feel* something to attain a goal is a *tactic*.)

CONCLUSION

> The printed script of a play is hardly more than an architect's blueprint of a house not yet built or built and destroyed. The color, the race and levitation, the structural pattern in motion, the quick interplay of live beings, these things are the play, not words on paper, not thoughts and ideas of the author (Tennessee Williams, Afterword to *Camino Real*).

Tennessee Williams' notion that the printed script guides a collaborative process is agreeable, though I do worry that this summary of a script's purpose may pave the way to some truly odd production choices. Rather, I would like you to think of a script as a *codebook for human behavior*. As the writer, it is up to you to create a behavioral guide that the actors can follow and play with in order to have an effect on the audience. The audience will decode the behavior and react accordingly. Keep in mind that it is up to you to make an audience *chase your play*. We do not want to spoon-feed them our ideas, our stories, because then they have no work to do. With the theatre, we want to entertain the audience, but we also want them to work. We want to create a lasting impression that they will take out into the world. One way we can achieve the goal of making the audience work is to create subtext via movements of the body instead of relying on characters to state the obvious.

CHAPTER *three*

CREATING DIALOGUE

Did you know we only listen to about 25-50% of what is actually said? In conversation, we often pause and feign listening because we are already thinking of what we want to say next, and we lose most of what people are actually saying to us. Authors are the great cultural pickpockets. We write based on what we observe and how we have processed our observations. We need to sharpen our listening skills and take in the world around us if we are going to write an insightful (and *inciteful*) letter to the world. Furthermore, our characters have to do a better job of listening to each other than we do in our day-to-day lives. Life is sporadic and odd, and most of our conversations don't have much purpose; theatre, even non-realist theatre, is rarely random, and when it is, there is still a purpose (revisit my thoughts on Dadaism in the introduction).

One of my favorite things to do was sit in public places and listen to people talk: coffee houses, airports, bus stations (especially fun!), and train stations (although, folks tend to hustle at train stations; not much time for conversation). I started writing down everything people say (again, in a public place) in order to fully understand the rhythms of human speech.

EXERCISE FIVE: OVERHEARD

In this exercise, I want you to sit in a public place and listen to a conversation. I want you to write down everything you hear verbatim. Any pauses, any stops, interruptions, etc. The best way to approach this task is to sit somewhere with a computer and your ear buds in. Make sure the conversation you write down is not spoken in whispers. Find some good, loud folks who seem to want the world to listen in to whatever is on their minds.

Here is an example of a scene that I wrote down while waiting at an airport. I had just spent the week in Valdez, Alaska at the Last Frontier Theatre Conference, one of the most rejuvenating experiences of my life. I wanted to write down everything that happened after such an exciting week. This scene involves two young men; one was on a cell phone relaying the conversation to his friend:

                        MAN IN YELLOW CAP
            Dude. Michael shaved his head.

                        GUY IN FLANNEL
            Shaved his head?

                        MAN IN YELLOW CAP
            Bic'd it.

                        GUY IN FLANNEL
            Bic'd it?

                        MAN IN YELLOW CAP
            Swear, broseph.

                        GUY IN FLANNEL
            Bic'd his head...

                        MAN IN YELLOW CAP
            Yeah.

                        GUY IN FLANNEL
            Wha-who did?

                        MAN IN YELLOW CAP
            Michael.

                        GUY IN FLANNEL
            Michael bic'd his head.

                        MAN IN YELLOW CAP
            Yeah, he—

                        GUY IN FLANNEL
            Wow.

```
                    MAN IN YELLOW CAP
Yeah.

                     GUY IN FLANNEL
That him now?

                    MAN IN YELLOW CAP
Yeah. Here.

    (Gives him the phone.)

                     GUY IN FLANNEL
You bic'd it?
```

This conversation is absolutely hilarious. This disbelief that Michael would bic his head, the constantly repeated information, the sense that the MAN IN YELLOW CAP was only half-listening, even while experiencing disbelief, created a strong comedic effect. I also noticed that there were stops, starts, interruptions. When you write down the conversation verbatim, make sure that you pick up all of the words.

For inspiration, be sure to visit the website Overheard in New York (www.overheardinnewyork.com). When we aren't paying attention to what we say—when we just talk to hear ourselves—it is absolutely wild what comes out of our mouths!

Here is an example from Louise Cook, who was a student of mine at the University of Georgia in Spring 2014. Notice how one person is controlling the conversation:

"SNOOPING EXERCISE" BY LOUISE COOK

```
    (It's about 11:30 on a Wednesday morning. There
    are two girls sitting in Starbucks. On the table
    between them is an open Bible, two journals, one
    cup of coffee, and a pen.)


                       GIRL 1
It's hard. Because you have to adjust. Sometimes you
just have to communicate at someone else's level.
Anyways I'm just saying this to sympathize with you.


                       GIRL 2
Ya.


                       GIRL 1
There's a lot of disappointment. This is gonna help.
They have tons of expectations for you. But they're
```

not your responsibility. Her happiness is not your problem.

(Pause.)

So…anyways. Pray with me. Father, thank you for this time. God, I ask that you bring sort of a resolution for the communication conflict between Erin and her family. God, if it's your desire to change Erin, I pray that you do change her and allow her to come to a place where she can release all of her worries. Lord, we thank you for your patience. I ask that you would speak clearly to Erin. That you would guide her and comfort her. That you encourage her heart in a way that is pleasing to you. In your powerful name, Amen. You're going to be okay. You will get through this. I wonder what's on the other side of this, ya know? Like, what is God trying to do on the other side of all this?

GIRL 2

Like, I think that right now it's just me having like misperceptions about it. And that will change but…I don't know. I guess that the way that I've been like, learning about God more recently…it hasn't been like the way that I've seen God on the mission trip I went to.

GIRL 1

Like Colombia?

GIRL 2

Ya. Like, it wasn't a waste of time but…I don't know. I didn't build any real relationships with people. I can't speak Spanish that well. Like, I don't know. I just didn't really feel…so. Ya, I don't know.

GIRL 1

I wonder if this is going to be different-like more skill building. Like sharpening your skills?

GIRL 2

Ya, I wonder. Like for Honduras. I would love to like, sit down with the people in the church and equip them more to be able to reach those people. Especially the things that I'm learning this semester, I feel like I have more of a perspective on missions…so…I don't know.

GIRL 1

What is the purpose? What are they going to do?

GIRL 2

Uhhh, I really haven't looked. That's why I just figure Honduras is like every other Spanish speaking country…like, they're all the same. But Honduras…like, their government opened their country up to Christian missionaries. They've opened the door for us so I'm sure there's things that God is doing there. Like they need people to help. But I feel like, with the call to go and make disciples of all nations, it's also teaching them to obey my commands, not just discipling them, ya know? I feel like that with time there…like, I feel like, yes, I can go but I would much rather equip the people that are there.

GIRL 1

Gotcha. I think that this is really interesting because I feel like God is beginning to clarify more like, where your desires are. He's speaking to you more. And that's gonna be really good. Part of the fruit will be you learning that. And its one more like…one more piece of guidance of the direction of your future. Like, what God's plan is for you and what he's put in your heart

GIRL 2

Ya.

GIRL 1

Really value this time as precious…

GIRL 2

Even with John North, he's like, "I want you to help me put together stuff for the athletes." And I'm like, I love athletes but I didn't play a sport so I don't feel entitled…you know the athletes need help. So if I could…I don't know. Honestly, I'd love people to take some of the things I'm doing this semester and unpack it in a smaller setting.

GIRL 1

Right.

GIRL 2

Ya.

GIRL 1

I think that as things get closer to going to Nashville and when you get to Nashville, I think that
you're just gonna need to be flexible and be okay
with doing a few things you don't really wanna do.
But then be able to verbalize it, like, "I don't
feel like I'm in my sweet spot when I'm doing this."

GIRL 2

And that's like…like, I feel like I'm prepared to
do that. When I say I'm not excited, I'm realizing
like, oh, there could be repercussions to this, not
so much I don't want to do this.

GIRL 1

Gotcha. Gotcha. Cool.

GIRL 2

So.

GIRL 1

So. I'm gonna get my coffee now. What do you have
going on the rest of the day?

GIRL 2

I have class and then I think I'm gonna go to the
DMV. I have to get a new license.

GIRL 1

When was your birthday?

GIRL 2

It was in December but I've been putting it off. But
today's the day because I really need a new license.
So I'll go there after class.

GIRL 1

Gotcha.
   (Silence.)
Okay well…I enjoyed it.

GIRL 2

Me too…thanks for preparing everything.

GIRL 1

Aw, you're welcome. Thanks for appreciating it.

(They stand. GIRL 1 looks at her phone.)
Oh. Oh my gosh. That's hilarious!

(They hug.)

                    GIRL 2
I love you.

                    GIRL 1
I love you too. Keep me updated.

(They walk away. End scene.)

Once again, notice how the people involved are not quite listening to one another. They also make some glaring mistakes, but in the natural flow of conversation, we tend to ignore false information out of not wanting to be rude, or out of not really listening.

Once you have your overheard conversation, consider how you might be able to massage it into your scene. Remember our "bic" scene? Here is how it played out in the beginning of my play *Attic Monster*, which received its world premiere at the GOOD Works Theatre Festival in Atlanta (directed by David Crowe). In this play, Frank and his younger wife Rory are sorting through boxes in the attic of Frank's childhood home. His mother has died, and he and his lay-about brother now must get the house ready to sell. We learn a bit about his brother, Gregory, who will be introduced shortly. I also incorporated part of one of my dreams in the scene:

(The opening to a song, such as "Duty Free" by Vic Chestnut, plays in the dark. LIGHTS UP. RORY and FRANK are looking over boxes in an attic. They have markers, tape, and cardboard boxes that aren't made up yet. They're in the middle of a conversation.)

                    RORY
Something happens to a woman's arms when she becomes a lesbian. They become longer; leaner. Maybe it's all the limbs. Stacey's neck looks longer, doesn't it? Doesn't Stacey's neck look longer?

(FRANK tapes a box shut.)

                    FRANK
Oh, I don't know.

                    RORY
I think it does. When my cousin Amy turned out to be

gay, I noticed it right away. (Beat). I'm not saying that they look ugly. I actually like really long
limbs. Plus, I'd totally go gay for Stacey, but you
know, I'm married. Plus she's getting married!

(FRANK looks at his arms. They are not particularly long. He turns away and looks over the boxes.)

What's the matter? I like your limbs, too!

                    FRANK
Nothing. I had a dream about Stacey last night.

                    RORY
Really? Was it hot?

                    FRANK
No, no. Well, I was driving along 9-W, and was about
to pass St. Anthony's Church. As I slowed down, I
noticed Stacey in the parking lot across the street,
walking towards the open doors. Now, Church was
in session, the congregation, erm, congregating on
the front lawn. A policeman was acting as crossing
guard. I saw Stacey, with her golden blonde hair all
long and unmanaged—

                    RORY
She cut it off.

                    FRANK
Really?

                    RORY
Yes. Bic'd it.

                    FRANK
Bic? Like?

(He motions as if shaving his head with a razor.)

                    RORY
Yeah. Bic'd.

                    FRANK
I can't imagine. (Beat). No! She had that hair,
that…you know…HAIR!

                              RORY
Not anymore. Longer arms, longer neck, balder head.

                              FRANK
Wow. WOW. (Beat). Wow.

                              RORY
You were saying?

                              FRANK
It doesn't matter, I guess. It really was just a
dream. Thought I was on an astral plane.

                              RORY
Astral plane, huh? What was so astral planey about
this dream?

                              FRANK
Well, I see her, and I park. She is moving strange-
ly. As if she had Parkinson's. I help her, literally, carrying her into the church. I let her walk as
we enter, and who is the priest, but Gregory.

                              RORY
Gregory?

                              FRANK
Yeah.

                              RORY
He said he'd catch fire if he ever set foot in a church.

                              FRANK
That would explain what happened next. We're about
to take communion. Now, I'm Methodist, so, it's off
limits for me. For one: alcohol. For two: Catholics
think they're actually drinking blood. It's a little vampiric. So, I help Stacey get to the cup, and
they're serving the wine out with a spoon. And the
wine isn't wine at all…it's grape Jello shots.

                              RORY
Jello shots?

                              FRANK
Yes. The blood of Christ wasn't wine, it was grape
Jello shots. Very bizarre.

                    RORY
And you thought this was real?

                    FRANK
Well, you know, in a "not really real, but kind of
real" sort of way.

                    RORY
Astral planey.

                    FRANK
Astral planey.

                    RORY
I know why you had that dream.

                    FRANK
Yeah?

                    RORY
Last time we saw Gregory and Stacey together, they
were at eighties night at Cabs. They got drunk and
argued all night about religion. Gregory said drinking Jello shots and dancing to Michael Jackson was
against his, and stormed out.

                    FRANK
That's funny.

                    RORY
(Beat.) You going to tell him?

                    FRANK
About the dream?

                    RORY
No. About Stacey.

                    FRANK
No. (Beat.) He'd just say sexuality is a continuum.
It won't bother him at all.

                    RORY
But it was serious with this girl.

     (FRANK is examining an ornament. End scene.)

The end scene comes from several sources: the conversation at the airport, a dream I once had, and my own personal circumstances following a sickness my mother had (though she thankfully recovered and is still with us). When you write, allow yourself to draw from a number of experiences in order to help your characters communicate your story to the audience.

REACTING

Have you ever heard the expression, "acting is reacting"? Sanford Meisner (1905-1997) was an early 20th century acting teacher who built the foundation of his theory on this principle. His key exercise was Repetition, often referred to as "a repeat." With the Repetition, two actors would sit very close (often with one of the actor's legs touching the other), and one of the partners would make an observation about the other acting partner, such as "your eyes are brown," or "you're wearing a green shirt," or "you have a mole on your chin." The two partners would repeat this line back and forth until some change was felt, and then the next line would be repeated.

Key to the Repetition was the partner's perspective/point of view. When one partner begins "your eyes are brown," the other partner reacts in a way that was truthful and open. As the repetition continues, the first acting partner, the one who observes "your eyes are brown," might notice the partner's point of view regarding their eyes, or it could be something else entirely, as long as the moment is truthful. With the Meisner Technique, each moment is grounded in absolute, spontaneous truth. The subtext is "lived" based on the actions between the characters, a step away from the Strasberg Method, in which actors were asked to mine personal circumstances in order to fuel a character's emotional need, which, some critics feel may keep performers living in an off-stage past rather than a very active present. For the Meisner-trained actor, each moment is created through a forward progression. We do not go back to "your eyes are brown" after the moment has changed. That was the past—what is happening in the present? What is happening in this moment? How does this moment create the next moment? And the next moment?

To clarify, I do not mean to suggest there isn't something to be learned from Method Acting. Our first exercise, dealing with photographs, is very much a Method-based approach. What I do want to do is suggest that there are a number of theatrical/acting techniques that can help us hone our skills as writers of drama.

EXERCISE SIX: LINE-THROUGH

As suggested last chapter, beginning writers often have characters talk in large chunks. The dialogue back-and-forth becomes a list of responses to the other character's thoughts, giving scenes a very choppy flow. With this exercise, the authors will learn how characters are reacting to each other in a way that is immediate and active. Each character brings with him or her a very personal perspective/point of view. I am going to give a brief, goofy example that will highlight how this exercise is supposed to work, so you will know how to incorporate it in your own scripts. In this scene, Bob and Jim will have a short conversation. The characters will repeat a previously spoken piece of dialogue as a question, before answering the question. It would look like this:

Step One: Write your dialogue.

>   BOB
> How are you, Jim?

>   JIM
> How am I? Great. Effin' great.

>   BOB
> Effin' great? Uh-oh.

>   JIM
> Uh-oh? Yeah. Don't want to get into it.

>   BOB
> Don't want to get into it? Fair enough.

>   JIM
> Fair enough? Thanks. What's that you're holding?

>   BOB
> What's this I'm holding? Here take this. I want you
> to have it.

>   JIM
> You want me to have it? Uhhh…okay. Thanks.

>   BOB
> Uhhh…okay, Thanks? You're welcome.

>   (Blackout.)

That was the first step in this exercise. Of course, as you write, your scenes should be a bit longer as you explore the organic truth between these characters.

Step Two: Strike through all the questions:

>   BOB
> How are you Jim?

>   JIM
> ~~How am I?~~ Great. Effin' great.

BOB

~~Effin great?~~ Uh-oh.

JIM

~~Uh-oh?~~ Yeah. Don't want to get into it.

BOB

~~Don't want to get into it?~~ Fair enough.

JIM

~~Fair enough?~~ Thanks. What's that you're holding?

BOB

~~What's this I'm holding?~~ Take this. I want you to have it.

JIM

~~You want me to have it?~~ Uhhh...okay. Thanks.

BOB

~~Uhhh...okay, Thanks?~~ You're welcome.

    (Blackout.)

Step three: Read it out loud. It should sound like this:

BOB

How are you Jim?

JIM

Great. Effin' great.

BOB

Uh-oh.

JIM

Yeah. Don't want to get into it.

BOB

Fair enough.

JIM

Thanks. What's that you're holding?

BOB

This is my past. I want you to have it.

                         JIM
Uhhh…okay. Thanks.

                         BOB
You're welcome.

    (Blackout.)

This is the end of the exercise. Again, I am offering a very goofy example, but I want to keep it simple for the sake of the exercise. As you move forward with your writing, find the organic truth to each interaction. You can find different ways for characters to move the story forward. Sometimes, a character might say nothing at all. For example, after Jim asks Bob, "How are you, Jim?" Jim might say nothing, which would also prompt Bob's "Uh-oh." There are other times when a monologue is absolutely necessary, but we are not there yet. For now, work on keeping your dialogue moving forward.

CONCLUSION

Writing dialogue can be incredibly challenging. Theatrical dialogue is ultimately a blend of heightened speech and natural speech. Learning the rhythms of natural speech can help you create authentic-sounding dialogue. Do keep in mind that however you go about creating your dialogue, you have an obligation to stick to your piece's internal logic. Also, it is quite okay to break your own rules as long as you do so in service to your world of story. For example, the dialogue in August Wilson's plays is quite sharp. He does layer his plays with a number of monologues that do not necessarily add to the forward progression of the play, but help create the world of story. These exercises offer a guideline to you as a beginning writer, but do not let them limit your imagination. Rather, if you find you are stuck, these are wonderful ways to stir your imagination and find your way out of a scene. Ultimately, you have something you want to say to the audience via your characters and their interactions. We want to make sure the message is clear.

Finally, one trick of the trade I've picked up: if both of your characters are talking too much (in your opinion), choose one to be your "person of few words." Think of Silent Bob in Kevin Smith's films. In most of the films he appears in, he only has one line of dialogue, so it is always a zinger. The same is true with false starts, "ums" and "ahs." Do use these, but use them sparingly and consistently for key characters.

CHAPTER *four*

ETHNOGRAPHY/JOURNALISM

Often, there is a notion that a playwright sits in isolation and waits for inspiration to strike. While this may be the case for some, there are many playwrights who actively seek inspiration by engaging with other works of art (as suggested with the photograph exercise in Chapter One), and still others who will hear a story in the news and travel to meet folks impacted by the events. The playwright will then act as both a journalist and ethnographer.

A journalist is someone who wishes to get the "facts" of a story; he or she is an impartial observer reporting the events. The ethnographer, on the other hand, will study a situation from the point of view of a subject impacted by the cultural moment. Broadly speaking, the ethnographer will study how meaning is made and how systems of communication work in a given culture (or cultural moment) from a more personal stance. Three of the most compelling dramas of the late 20th century—*The Exonerated, Fire in the Mirrors,* and *The Laramie Project*—rely on the playwright performing the roles of journalist and ethnographer.

With *The Exonerated* (2002), playwrights Jessica Blank and Erik Jensen interviewed innocent people who had been on death row. They additionally culled material from other sources (interviews, transcripts, and personal letters) in order to create a 90-minute play that successfully showed the human side to a deeply divisive death penalty conversation. The playwrights relied on the words and movement of the exonerated to create a journalistic piece of theatre. However, the writers were by no means detached. We are given the facts of the story, but in a way that gives the strongest emotional response to incredibly dire circumstances.

With *The Laramie Project* (2000), Moises Kaufman and the Members of the Tectonic Theatre Project visited Laramie, Wyoming following the 1998 murder of gay college student, Matthew Shepard. The mission of the Tectonic Theatre Project gives me pause: "A theatre company travels *somewhere*, talks to people, and *returns* with what it saw and heard to create a play" (vi). Kaufman's approach to writing combines journalism and ethnography with a touch of drama critic and director, and Bertolt Brecht's idea of "The Street Scene," which Kaufman points to as his inspiration for the "creation" and "aesthetic vocabulary" of this play (vi-vii). As Kaufman suggests, "The Street Scene" is Brecht's "model of 'an eyewitness demonstrating to a collection of people how a traffic accident took place'" (Kaufman, vii). The Tectonic Theatre Project writes and performs in their plays, a marked difference from the approach used by Jessica Blank and Erik Jensen, who had six actors perform their play in its initial run at Bleecker St. Theatre in 2002.

Another example of playwright as journalist/ethnographer is Anna Deavere Smith, whose *Fires in the Mirror* documents racial tension between members of the Hasidic Jewish and African-American communities in a neighborhood in Brooklyn, New York. In 1991, a Hasidic Rabbi's motorcade hit and killed a young African-American boy, and in retaliation, a young Jewish student from Austria was killed. The tension escalated, as Smith notes, because of the role of the police, who were "seen as pervasive and oppressive by Black people," and "ineffective and absent by the Lubavitchers" (xxxv). Smith took it upon herself to interview a number of people who lived in that neighborhood, as well as more media-visible faces, such as Reverend Al Sharpton. From these interviews, Smith created a theatrical work that does not push empathetic or cathartic buttons in her audience. Rather, a problem is given a voice—many voices, in fact—without a resolution. It is up to the audience to determine what the web of violence and racial tension means.

Smith conducted each interview and played each character herself. She says in her introduction, "My goal was to create an atmosphere in which the interviewee would experience his/her own authorship. Speaking teaches us what our natural 'literature' is" (Smith, xxxi). By using this ethnographic approach, Smith argues she can "create the illusion of being another person by reenacting something they had said *as they had said it*" (Smith, xxvi). Furthermore, she believed in the power of reenactment, not mimicry, and believed that it "could tell us as much, if not more, about another individual than the process of learning about the other by using the self as a frame of reference" (xxvii). In other words, like the journalist, Smith attempts to remain neutral by presenting the interviews verbatim—verbally and physically.

48

The three very different approaches used by Blank and Jensen, Kaufman and the Members of the Tectonic Theatre, and Anna Deavere Smith, rely on the playwright's ability to engage in a nuanced conversation with a community that has been divided by a major cultural event. These plays, in turn, act as a microcosm for a much bigger national conversation. In other words, a "local" conversation may become "global." This is an incredibly daunting task, as the writer is responsible for all of the voices involved in creating the play. When discussing how his words will be used in *The Laramie Project*, Father Roger Schmit says to company members that he does not want his words to be used to instigate or support "violence, even in its smallest form" (66). What he offers to the theatre company is something we can all learn from: "Just deal with what is true. You know what is true. You need to do your best to say it correct" (66).

TALKING TO PEOPLE

One of the most rewarding theatre experiences for me as a writer was a project I co-authored with Keith Dorwick called *NIGHTFEARS*. A mixed media play, *NIGHTFEARS* was developed through 21 interviews with people in the Acadiana region of Louisiana. Asked to talk about their fears, the interviews were the source (in part) for the material that appeared on three large video screens at the back of the set. A cast of four (Lexie Carroll, Michael Cato, Casey Harmon, and Josey Toups) presented material from the interviews in ways that underscore the pervasive fear that we all face as we attempt to cope with such realities as disease, death, war, and various kinds of financial insecurity as well as the childhood fears we never really outgrow. Some of the scenes were transcripts from the interviews, while others incorporated moments of dance and dream-like movement to underscore a particular thought or mood.

Because working on this play introduced new approaches to writing for me, I want you to try a couple of exercises based on this process. Creating a play based on interviews really freed up my imagination! Furthermore, this process, like the overheard exercise in the last chapter, gave me a better understanding of the rhythms of human speech, and how we use words in our day-to-day conversations. What I learned from doing this has helped me create naturalistic dialogue in all of my plays, whether the plays are realistic or not.

Exercise Seven: Interview

I want you to ask someone, someone who you trust, if you can interview them. Ask them one of the following questions and just let them talk. Feel free to follow up with another question or two, or three, if they start heading into interesting territory. Let them know that you plan on using this interview for an exercise that could become a play. You may change their name in the play itself for the sake of privacy, or, if they are willing to sign a release, you may use their name in the finished work.

1. What really keeps you awake at night? Why? What is the worst thing that could happen?
2. What is your favorite song? When was the last time you heard it? What happened? What does this song remind you of?
3. What have you done after you've had your heart broken? Were you surprised? What did you do after that? What have you done since?
4. What was your favorite childhood toy? What is your favorite memory dealing with this toy?
5. What was your favorite home-cooked meal? When was the last time you had this meal? What does this meal remind you of?

After the interview, create a scene—it can be abstract, it can be realistic, it can play with time; it can incorporate only what the interviewee said, or it can be an impressionistic piece based on a single moment in the interview.

EXERCISE EIGHT: AMALGAM SCENE

After you have completed Exercise Seven, go back and look at your interview again. Then, look at your overheard exercise. Use these two exercises to create a new scene. You may draw from elements of the conversations, you may use pieces of the conversation verbatim. Just please, don't make it a scene about someone being interviewed. Do something else—something entirely different using the interview and overheard discussion as raw material. Your finished piece may be abstract or it could be realistic. Either is absolutely fine. Remember, the theatre is an abstract space, so if this scene is not realistic, that really is okay. I know some of the exercises we've performed so far might lend themselves more to Realism, but this does not mean you need to only write domestic dramas. Open up your imagination and enjoy!

CONCLUSION

The playwright is the great cultural pickpocket. We find inspiration from other works of art and from other people. While some approaches to writing ask us to quietly tune out the world so we can hear what our inner voices are trying to tell us, there are other approaches to writing which ask us to actively engage with other people in order to tell their stories honestly and respectfully. Additionally, these conversations may inspire other pieces of writing. Whatever story you decide to tell, make sure to approach the story respectfully and responsibly. Our greatest responsibility, as writers, is to respectfully engage with other people.

CHAPTER *five*

FAMILIAR/UNFAMILIAR

Have you ever heard the saying that art is supposed to make the familiar strange, or the familiar unfamiliar? This is a theory that comes from literary critic and Russian Formalist Victor Shklovsky. In his essay, "Art as Technique," Shklovsky argues:

> The purpose of art is to impart the sensation of things as they are perceived and not as they are known. The technique of art is to make objects "unfamiliar," to make forms difficult, to increase the difficulty and length of perception because the process of perception is an aesthetic end in itself and must be prolonged. Art is a way of experiencing the artfulness of an object: the object is not important... (Shklovsky).

The act of defamiliarization or *estrangement* has been a valuable tool for the theatre artist. Bertolt Brecht's (1898-1956) approach to Epic Theatre relies on the ability to make known objects (as well as culturally agreed upon ideas) unfamiliar. If we were to watch a play written and/or directed by Brecht, we would see placards with the title of the scene; we would see actors who were not relying on their own personal histories to create characters, but rather caricatures, as if the actors were playing their roles in quotation marks. For Brecht, the idea was to think above the play, rather than to be lulled into lazy emotional responses (see "Introduction" for more on Brecht's theatre). Although Brecht was interested in pushing a social agenda (inciting the audience to be agents of change), I believe we can use the idea of making the familiar unfamiliar in all of our writing, whether or not we have Shklovsky's aesthetic agenda or Brecht's desire to foreground the problems of economic class systems.

One wonderful example of getting around exposition using a familiar/unfamiliar approach comes from an anecdote in Blake Snyder's screenwriting book, *Save the Cat!* In his section "Pope in the Pool," Snyder remembers:

> Mike Cheda told me about a script he once read called, *The Plot to Kill the Pope*, by George Englund, which did a very smart thing. It's basically a thriller. And the scene where we learn the details of the vital backstory goes like this: Representatives visit the Pope at the Vatican pool. There, the Pope, in his bathing suit, swims laps back and forth while the exposition unfolds. We, the audience, aren't even listening, I'm guessing. We're thinking: "I didn't know the Vatican had a *pool*? And look, the Pope's not wearing his Pope clothes, he's…he's…in his bathing suit!" And before you can say, "Where's my miter?" the scene's over (124).

Setting the meeting at a pool made the scene much more engaging than it would have been had the writer decided to set it in an office. This scene, which offers important exposition, excites the audience and makes them ask a series of questions simply by making the familiar (The Pope and swimming) unfamiliar. This is a key idea for the writer: in order to *incite* our audience, we must *engage* with them; we want them to ask questions along the way. If the audience is not asking questions, then we are not fully involving them.

EXERCISE NINE: FAMILIAR/UNFAMILIAR

In this exercise, you will create a scene in which two characters enter a space. The first uses the space for its intended use. The second character will use the space for a different purpose. The characters will have a conversation that has nothing to do with the activity. Here are the steps:

1. Character A enters a space and uses it for its intended purpose.
2. Character B enters a space and uses it for something other than its intended purpose.
3. Characters A and B have a discussion in which Character B's bizarre activity is not spoken about.

This exercise presents us with another way of getting around exposition: if someone is using a space in a new way and neither comment on this behavior, we understand that not only is this odd behavior part of the second character's make-up, but that the first character has gotten so used to the second character's bizarre behavior that it no longer surprises him or her. This can speak volumes about their relationships in a way that is active, strange, and that avoids long, expository passages.

For example, writer William N. Dunlap wrote a scene in which a young man is practicing a trombone in a music rehearsal room on a college campus. We hear a couple enter a rehearsal room next door. They begin having sex. The trombone player attempts to practice. The characters having sex stop for a moment to discuss who it could be in the next room. They decide it doesn't matter, and they continue having sex. The trombone player keeps practicing; at times, the sliding of his trombone and the sound that it produces coincide with the couple. This was one of the funniest scenes I had read in a long time, and a great use of using a space for something other than its intended purpose. Furthermore, as the trombone player was not only not having sex, but desperately trying to practice despite the noises in the next room, we could draw some conclusions about him as well: dedicated to his craft at the expense of social/romantic activities.

In a short scene I wrote for Next Stage Press's anthology *64 Squares*, a young man stands at a mirror brushing his teeth. Another a young man enters, fully dressed, carrying a brown bag of groceries. This second young man turns on the tub water, gets in, and begins cutting up a carrot while fully dressed in the bath. Their conversation focuses on the trials and tribulations of love. Neither discusses the odd bathtub behavior. What conclusions can we draw from these two characters? How well do they know each other? Does the second character do these strange activities so much that the first character is inured? Or, could it be that the first character is so self-absorbed that he's not even noticing his roommate's (possible) breakdown? As the scene progresses, these questions are answered, but the hope is that an audience member watching or reading the play will be hooked by the bizarre use of space.

CONCLUSION

The familiar/unfamiliar exercise can be quite helpful when trying to problem-solve a moment in your script. I once had a student who insisted on writing a relationship play in a coffee house. He wanted to show how selfish individuals can be when trying to negotiate their way into (or out of) a romantic/sexual relationship. After several attempts, I recommended he try moving the setting of his play to a funeral parlor, during the viewing hours, over an open casket of a nine-year-old girl. (I know…dark. But the characters certainly read as self-involved!) Another student wrote a scene in which a teenage girl tells her parents that she's pregnant. The style was realistic and the genre was seriocomedy. We talked about how we could mix up the scene a bit. I recommended she set it in a library near the desk of a very elderly librarian (male) who insisted on absolute quiet. The result was poignant and hilarious, relying on characters to pantomime much of what they wanted to say.

When you feel stuck, remember, your script is trying to get the audience to see familiar situations in a new way. It is up to you to figure out how you can take life's familiar moments and make them fresh, new. Unfamiliar. Your imagination is the limit.

CHAPTER *six*

WRITING ADAPTATIONS

This chapter will be a little different than our previous chapters as the subject of "adaptations" can be a book unto itself. I have participated with a number of round-tables and panels where we have discussed adaptation theory in the theatre, and most of the plays I write are adaptations. In fact, I think the argument could be made that everything I write is an adaptation, or at the very least, an appropriation. On a few occasions (mostly weddings with non-theatre folks) I've ended up having this conversation: Potential Friend: "What do you do?" Me: "I'm a playwright." Potential Friend: "Oh! What kind of plays?" Me: "Mostly adaptations." Then, there is a silence. After a moment, Potential Friend: "hey, that's great, though. I mean, all you have to do is take the dialogue and add a few stage directions?" Me: (not sure what to say) "Ha, yes." And I walk away. What I have learned from these conversations is writing adaptations is cheating, somehow not an art in-and-of-itself (unless copying-and-pasting is considered art).

Most persons working in the theatre understand that theatre itself is an art of adaptation: that is, written words are being performed by live bodies in space. The two dimensions of the page are adapted to meet the three dimensions of the body in space. Playwrights also understand that all plays are, to some extent, adaptations, relying on the writer's own encounters with the world, with other works of art, with other scripts, and with various media for storytelling. There is an understanding of audience expectations within a given genre. If I tell someone I am going to see the new *Star Trek* film, the other person—even if he or she has no experience with *Star Trek*—can make assumptions based on the title: a work of science fiction, set in space, involving travel and exploration, and the trials and tribulations that come with encountering new cultures. So why are writers of direct adaptation the elephant in the room? I am really not sure what the answer to this question is; but I can discuss different approaches to adaptations and talk about my own experience, which might be helpful (or at least inspire confidence) to those wishing to write plays inspired by other works.

First, we should agree that there are different "types" of adaptation: there are "direct" adaptations, which are usually judged via the "fidelity" test (how close is it to the source material?); there are translations (one language into another, often with new phrases in order to deal with regionalisms and colloquialisms); there are postdramatic works (such as Wooster Group's *LSD*, a pastiche which draws on/deconstructs a number of known works and ideologies); and there are language-based-adaptations, which fall into one of two categories: 1) Works that keep the story intact but foreground a philosophical question grounded in a current context (Neal Bell's *Monster*, an adaptation of Mary Shelley's *Frankenstein* is an example), or 2) Works that appropriate known cultural tropes, character types, or rely on an audience's knowledge with genre in order to pose questions in a current cultural, socioeconomic context (Len Jenkin's *Dark Ride* is an example).

Direct adaptations can be the most tricky to pull off: in recent research with humanoid androids, it has been noted that faces which look the most human come off as the most uncanny/unnerving as subtle details—such as blinking—have not been perfected; as a result the more "human" the android, the more grotesque. This can often be the case with writing a "direct" adaptation. Audiences often only see the differences, rather than the similarities. This is not to say that there are no effective direct adaptations (Romulus Linney's adaptation of Ernest Gaines' *A Lesson Before Dying* is a very strong work), rather my suggestion is that a faithful adaptation is easy prey for the "fidelity" argument: If the work is too faithful, it is considered pointless and derivative; if it is not completely faithful, devotees to the source material will call it flawed.

Postdramatic works tend to have a built-in audience, mostly avant-gardists and academics, and theatre practitioners operating in the New York Independent Theatre. I, in no way, mean to write these works off, as I tend to love postdramatic theatre, but rather to say that they are coded/read by different audiences then, say, those who embrace the Harry Potter film franchise. In other words, postdramatic theatre audiences have their own expectations for the work they are about to receive: a destabilizing of the text for the sake of the image/aesthetic/political message (especially for works which claim there are no politics involved).

Because I was mentored by a language playwright (Neal Bell), my adaptations tend to be language-based. My play, *Hound* (produced Off-Off Broadway, directed by Rachel Klein), is an adaptation of *The Hound of the Baskervilles*. It was produced in 2009, just before the Hollywood *Sherlock Holmes* and new BBC/Steven Moffat series. I wrote *Hound* after reading Bell's *Monster*. I was on the phone with him, and we were discussing his play, when the conversation turned to *The Hound of the Baskervilles*, which I had recently re-read. I told him I was unsatisfied with most of the film and stage adaptations that already existed. There was so much more to the characters, and to the writing of the novel, which often gets lost under a deerstalker cap and in the smoke of a curved pipe.

The Hound of the Baskervilles was the first Holmes story Doyle penned after killing off his famous sleuth. Doyle was given the idea for the story from a friend, and considered creating a new detective to solve the case. Doyle decided since he had a detective already, he would simply set the story prior to Holmes' death. This, along with Gillette's successful melodrama *Sherlock Holmes*, would lead *Strand Magazine* to make a deal with Doyle to bring Holmes back from the dead. Holmes would emerge from Reichenbach Falls in "The Adventure of The Empty House." In order to bring Holmes and Watson back to their living quarters at 221B Baker Street, Doyle did sacrifice Watson's wife, Mary (Morstan) Watson, and he did so without mentioning her name! In "The Empty House," Holmes tells Watson how he survived his fall with Moriarty, and gives his reasons why he decided to fake his death. Watson then tells the reader:

> In some manner he [Holmes] had learned of my own sad bereavement, and his sympathy was shown in his manner rather than in his words. 'Work is the best antidote to sorrow, my dear Watson,' said he; 'and I have a piece of work for us both to-night which, if we can bring it to a successful conclusion, will in itself justify a man's life on this planet (Doyle, "The Adventure of the Empty House").

That was all the grieving Watson was allowed, as the game was afoot.

I mentioned this to Bell, and told him how I would write a stage version of *The Hound of the Baskervilles*, making it the first case Watson and Holmes collaborate on post-Empty House in order to give Watson time to grieve. I suggested I would give the play a treatment similar to his take on Shelley's novel, and he charged me to start writing it immediately.

With Doyle's book next to my arm, I began typing, occasionally glancing in. After a short time, I gave up looking in the book altogether, and strange things started happening: the working class citizens, those ignored by the key characters, starting talking to the audience, explaining why they must continue to do what they do; Watson suddenly had the ability to communicate with dogs (I almost deleted his first conversation with the Curly Haired Spaniel—frankly, I worried it might be too farfetched), and I allowed Watson to grieve. In the novel, a Hell Hound plagues the Baskerville family, and the last of the line is prophesied to meet his doom via the hound as his Uncle had before him. Holmes plants Watson in Dartmoor—as a distraction—while he solves the case behind the scenes. When the Hound turns out to be a ruse, the characters feel vindicated that reason, justice, and the empirical world has won out over superstitions. In my play, Watson is not planted by Holmes; rather, he insists that he needs to venture to the moor in order to meet this Hell Hound, learn of the afterlife, and see his dead wife once again. And when the Hound turns out to be a normal dog, beaten and controlled by a very human adversary, ruse? Watson loses his faith. However, he will continue working with Holmes, for he is a sidekick, and that is what sidekicks do.

The play was a success with audiences and with critics, and was eventually published with Next Stage Press and on Indie Theatre Now. Most important for me, it was a success because I was able to keep Doyle's framework intact, and keep the characters of Holmes and Watson consistent with the stories (at least, I felt the characters were consistent; they trust each other entirely, even if they get on one another's nerves).

Writing an adaptation can be very helpful for those who struggle with plot structure: there is a clear beginning, middle, and end. However, what the writer needs to consider are the following questions:

1. Why do I need to (re)tell this story?
2. How can the stage foreground themes intended by the author vary, as well as themes that are more current for theatre audiences?
3. Who is this adaptation for? (I always consider an audience.)
4. What can I add to the life and legacy of these characters?

If you are writing an adaptation simply because you enjoyed a book, you might end up painting yourself into a corner by trying to keep everything from the book intact (the fidelity argument!). Give yourself the freedom to use the source material as a platform from which you can launch into your own story, your own adventure, and your own questions you want to pose to the universe. Like I said, performance is a three-dimensional medium, and a novel can do things that a playscript simply cannot. The reverse is true as well: embrace that difference. Finally, when you find yourself at a party and a Potential Friend asks what do you do, tell them "I write for the theatre," and invite Potential Friend to see your play. Perhaps it is best to avoid the awkward conversation altogether.

EXERCISE TEN: MASH-UP

Because television and film have dominated the realistic, well-made aesthetics, the question is regularly asked, "what can plays do differently?" The language-based writers of the late 20th century have answered this question by creating works which rely on literary and cultural archetypes in order to foreground a philosophical question. Writers of Geek Theatre in the 21st century have created plays tailored for the "Geek audience," a subcultural group with an uncanny love for SciFi/Fantasy, comic books, table-top and other role-playing games, CosPlay, etc. With this exercise, writers will be asked to create a pastiche: a work that borrows heavily from known tropes in order to create something new. The work created in this exercise will be referential and self-conscious. It may be campy. It may be dramatic. It may be both! At the heart of it, some philosophical question must be asked.

1. Read a comic book.
2. Play a table-top role-playing game.
3. Play an 8-bit video game (you can find plenty online).
4. Write down three experiences the central character faces in each of these adventures—consider the character's quest and what he or she wants to attain.
5. Rewrite the quest in a modern-day, realistic setting. Perhaps your central character wants a cup of coffee (the elixir they will need to give them strength to battle the Big Boss at the end), but they must face the first Boss: the Barista who gets the order wrong.

Have fun with this exercise. There is really no wrong way to approach it. Furthermore, feel free to create moments that may rely on media: sound effects, projections. There is no limit!

CONCLUSION: PASTICHE AND POSTMODERN PLAYWRITING

In this chapter, I mentioned postdramatic theatre, which is a form of theatre that decenters the importance of the script (see "Introduction). The events are much more visual, and in most cases, any sense of a linear plot with defined characters is abandoned. Take a moment and do a web-search on the theatre of Robert Wilson. Look at the imagery he creates.

When we talk about postmodern playwriting, I want you to understand that we no longer have to confine ourselves to dialogue. Broadly speaking (quite broadly, really), theories in the category of post-structuralism invite us to view all that we "see" as a text to be read, with the interpretation of each text being different for each whom encounter it (see Roland Barthes' "The Death of the Author" and Michel Foucault's "What is an Author?"). While these theories are dense (and often, philosophers labeled as "post-structuralists" are actually at odds with one another), what this means for us as writers is that we do not have to rely on the notion that words (i.e., dialogue) are our only source of text. That is not to say there is something wrong with our spoken and written language; rather, that our insistence that language be the primary mode of communication, that actors must speak the speech in order to make objectives understood, that there even needs to be "objectives" to begin with, is removed or diminished in order to experience not a catharsis, but a sublimation. When postdramatic auteur Robert Wilson sketches a set, he is writing. When Richard Foreman decides to keep the props the same size as the actors, he is writing. When innovative director Peter Brook decides to bring in a trapeze to create circus magic for *A Midsummer Night's Dream*, he is writing. What I am suggesting to you is we have the ability to create a world of images. We are still relying on structures and patterns in regard to how the words appear on the page: we are using stage directions to give both visual and emotional cues. However, it is quite alright to say in your stage directions, "the night grabs the audience by the crotch." We can talk about what that might mean, and how we can create that sensation (without physically grabbing crotches).

If we wish to blend the postmodern with narrative (something Sam Shepard excels at), we can say, "the Southwest as imagined by Edward Hopper." How will that inspire the imagination of both the reader and the lighting designer who have the opportunity to work with your play? And yet, you may still create an aesthetic unity even if you never wish the audience to feel completely comfortable. As Pulitzer Prize-winning playwright Paula Vogel once said of her play, *How I Learned to Drive*, "What I really hope is we enjoy, and laugh, and get closer being uncomfortable together" (Second Stage Theatre). Consider taking this hope with you as you embark on your writing.

CHAPTER *seven*

WORST. PLAY. EVER.

I closed the last chapter asking you to allow the audience to feel uncomfortable. Now, it is your turn! This exercise is simple: you've tried a bunch of these exercises, you've read my thoughts on what playwrights should be doing and how plays can be structured. I want you now to write a bad play. It can be five pages, ten pages. If you're really ambitious, go ahead and make it a full one-act. Whatever "bad play" means to you. Go ahead and do that. Don't even think. Just write. When your characters start talking, ask yourself, "what's the worst thing they can say right now?" Ask yourself, "what can't possibly be staged?" Ask yourself, "how far can this moment go?" Just be big and be bad. Be fearless and terrible.

EXERCISE ELEVEN: WORST PLAY EVER

Steps:
1. Write a bad play.

CONCLUSION

At the end of our playwriting section in my introduction to dramatic writing courses, I close with this exercise. All of your inhibitions should come barreling out. Your "bad play" might be boring. It might be impossible to stage. It might be incredibly violent. It might be loaded with cusses. However, somewhere in there is a gem. There might be a line, a passage, a thought, an image, or something that really got you going. As suggested earlier, many plays are pastiches. Often, I find inspiration by pretending I have an allergy to the backspace button. This has led to a lot of terrible writing, but there's always something I can use later. Another way to look at what you have created through these exercises is a bunch of parts: it is up to you to Frankenstein them together (yes, I'm using "Frankenstein" as a verb). I keep a folder of scenes, ten-minutes, monologues, and sketches that I have rejected. Many of them have been used in other plays. Some are still waiting to be used. Sometimes, I write with the only purpose of keeping this folder brimming with cringe-worthy material. If it is our job to take the familiar and make it unfamiliar, to make the audience feel close in their discomfort, we need to take incredibly bold risks with our writing. If you feel embarrassed to be around yourself right now, then you have succeeded in the exercise. Hold onto this bad play. Something may come of it!

Another reason why I believe this exercise is so important is because by breaking "the rules," we demonstrate that we know the rules; and by purposely writing something "bad," the anxiety to create something "good" dissipates, leading to unfiltered honestly on the stage. Some of the best short plays I have read began as "Worst. Plays. Ever." You, as writers, now know the rules—now you need to have fun!

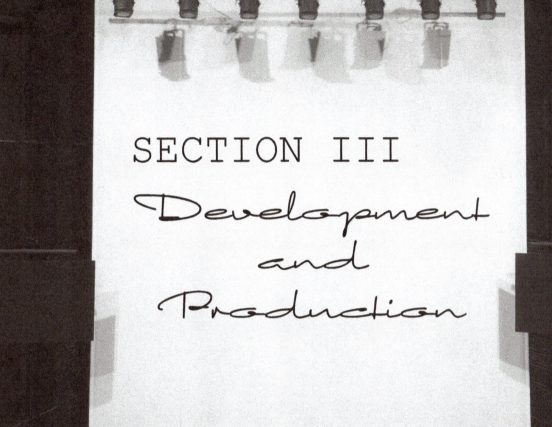

SECTION III

Development and Production

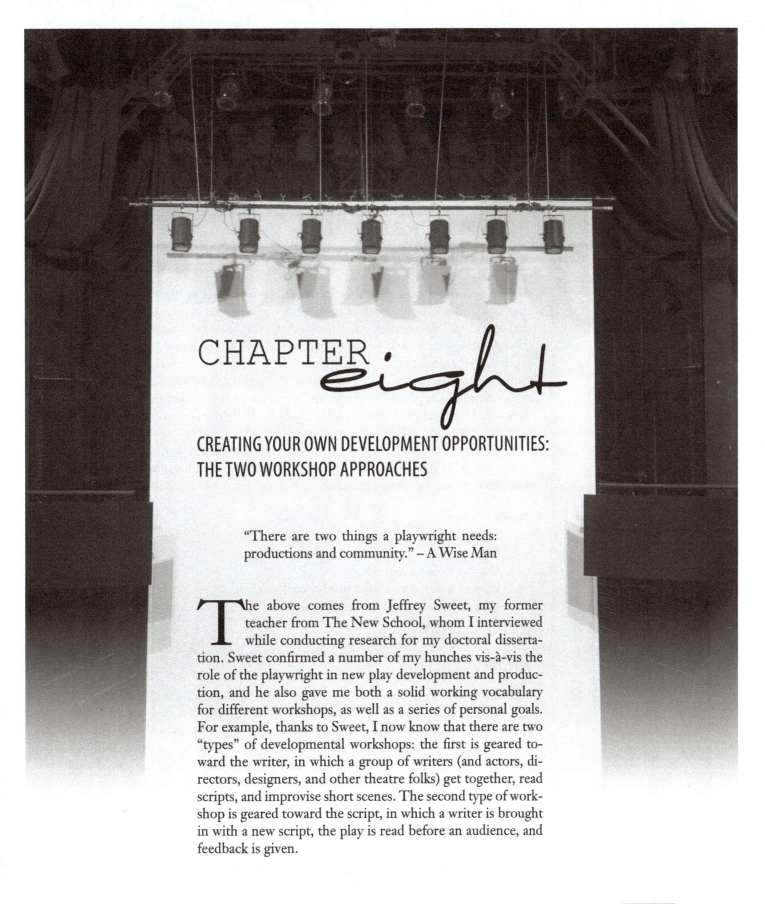

CHAPTER *eight*

CREATING YOUR OWN DEVELOPMENT OPPORTUNITIES: THE TWO WORKSHOP APPROACHES

"There are two things a playwright needs: productions and community." – A Wise Man

The above comes from Jeffrey Sweet, my former teacher from The New School, whom I interviewed while conducting research for my doctoral dissertation. Sweet confirmed a number of my hunches vis-à-vis the role of the playwright in new play development and production, and he also gave me both a solid working vocabulary for different workshops, as well as a series of personal goals. For example, thanks to Sweet, I now know that there are two "types" of developmental workshops: the first is geared toward the writer, in which a group of writers (and actors, directors, designers, and other theatre folks) get together, read scripts, and improvise short scenes. The second type of workshop is geared toward the script, in which a writer is brought in with a new script, the play is read before an audience, and feedback is given.

Athens Playwrights' Workshop (APW) is an example of the former. For two years, we have been meeting on alternate Monday nights at the University of Georgia, eating donuts and cupcakes, and sharing scripts. Every Monday night I make new discoveries as a playwright, teacher, and "fan" of new work. This year (2012-2013) I was delighted that three of the plays found productions with student organizations.

HOW TO CREATE A PLAYWRIGHT-LED WORKSHOP

According to choreographer Liz Lerman, every workshop has three key roles: the artist, who "offers a work in progress for review and is prepared to question that work in a dialogue with other people;" the responder(s), who are "committed to supporting the artist's intent to make excellent work [and to] engage in dialogue with the artist;" and the facilitator (whom I refer to as the moderator), who "initiates each step, keeps the process on track, and works to help the artist and responders use the process to frame useful questions and responses" (Lerman and Borstel). These definitions are spot-on and should help you as you move forward with getting your workshop on track.

Here are some very basic steps to starting a playwright-led, writer-centered workshop. This is an approach that has worked for me and for others, so do consider each step as you move forward:

Steps:
1. Find people.
2. Get a space.
3. Discover your dynamics.
4. Choose a different moderator for each session.
5. Give honest, but not brutal, feedback.
6. Everyone eats.

FINDING PEOPLE

The key to finding people is pretty simple—ask! If you are attending a college or university, visit playwriting courses and ask fellow students if they would like to create a workshop with you. If you are not attending (or otherwise involved with) a college or university, visit local theatres and see if they have new play festivals. See if anyone is local. Write to local actors, directors, and writers and see if they are interested in starting a twice-a-month workshop. You will be surprised how many people show an interest.

GET A SPACE

If you are a student, see if you can sign out a space on campus. Otherwise, consider hosting a get-together at your apartment. If you do not have your own space, look into community venues, including the lobby of community theatres during one of their dark nights. Just ask! Some places might say, "no," but you will eventually get a "yes." Be creative—do you know someone who works at the firehouse? At the library? At a bagel shop? You will find the right space.

DISCOVER YOUR DYNAMICS

During your first meeting, do a few exercises together from this book as an introduction and just have fun. With the first meeting you will be able to figure out your dynamics. You will also be able to figure out who will come back the following meeting and who might just be there because their interest was piqued. With the Athens Playwrights' Workshop, we began with fifteen people. We currently have a core group of six, with four others who drift in-and-out during the academic year.

CHOOSE A DIFFERENT MODERATOR FOR EACH SESSION

This is one of the most important components to any workshop. There needs to be someone in the role of leader. However, you do not want to become stuck with a single dynamic in which one person is in charge and the rest have to follow. In *The Dramatist's Toolkit*, Jeffrey Sweet recounts how he formed The New York Writers' Bloc during the late 1970s as a response to the single-moderator approach to the Actors Studio's Playwrights Unit (PU). At the PU, Sweet suggests that moderator Israel Horovitz had created a power dynamic in which the other members felt lesser-than Horovitz, to the point that members were worried about making comments during the feedback session. Sweet's group, The New York Writers' Bloc, was meant to be more democratic. However, Sweet had held the reigns so long that other members were worried that The Bloc would become a shadow of the PU. Sweet remembers:

> After awhile, there was a bloodless coup; I was toppled from my throne as head of the Bloc and demoted to an equal. After licking my bruised ego, I was delighted to find myself one of a band of friends who continued to meet for almost ten years (*The Dramatist's Toolkit*, 148).

I strongly believe the lesson learned by Sweet should be one that we as writers embrace. If we want to form our own workshops, we have to trust each other and allow each member of a group to take the lead. Rotate the moderator as much as possible just to keep everything on an even keel. With the APW, George Pate (then a doctoral student at UGA) was co-moderator. After awhile, I turned the reigns over to other students and graduates. The result was an environment of camaraderie and good will while creating our art.

GIVE HONEST, BUT NOT BRUTAL, FEEDBACK

I've heard a lot of great ideas about how to give feedback. When David Staller ran the Epic Rep. reading series at The Players' Club, he often told responders not to say what they loved or didn't love; if responders say they loved something, playwrights might not think they loved it enough, and wouldn't listen; and if responders said they didn't love (or even like) something, the playwright would think they had missed the point of the piece and wouldn't listen. Staller has an incredible wit and remains one of the most charming men I have ever met, so he could get away with saying anything he wanted about playwrights—especially since it was all said with love. I do think there is value to the suggestion that we avoid using the terms "liked" or "loved" when discussing a piece in process. Lanford Wilson and Dawson Moore created guidelines for the Last Frontier Theatre Conference, which includes the following:

- Pose observations, don't offer solutions.
- A writer needs to know when you were engaged and when you were not.
- Your positive response is most helpful, while your negative response is not.
- This is a nurturing environment, though you do not need to coddle the writers.
- Do not offer rewrite suggestions. Do not rewrite the play. Do not make it what you think it should be.
- Whether you liked or disliked the play is irrelevant to your response (Moore and Wilson).

Perhaps the most popular approach to critical response comes from choreographer Liz Lerman. Frustrated by giving and receiving criticism over the years, Lerman developed a four-step process for giving and receiving feedback (Moore and Wilson).

EVERYONE EATS

This is how I attracted folks to the first APW meeting who might not have otherwise attended. I promised donuts. I promised cookies. After the first few weeks one of our core members, Jennie Czuba, started baking for our meetings. Another one of our core members, Jordana Rich, started bringing cookies and cupcakes. Promise food and folks will attend!

As you move forward with your playwright-led/writer-centered workshop, realize that you are entering a journey with a group of people who will be very active in your artistic process, and potentially your day-to-day life. You are building relationships as you create your work. As you move forward, it is possible that feathers might get ruffled—that is part of the process. Keep rotating moderators and remember you are all here for the same thing: to focus on your individual voices, to make sure that when you want to Say Something to an audience, you know the best way to say it. That is what makes this style of workshop writer-centered rather than script-centered.

A few paragraphs ago, I mentioned the New York Writers' Bloc. I want to take a few pages and discuss the group. My hope is that by providing this case study, you can see for yourself how easy it is to create your own development opportunity, and as a happy byproduct, you can create your own community of artists.

In the 1960s, Off-Off Broadway emerged in the coffee houses and found spaces in the name of forming artistic communities. In the unfortunately out-of-print *Off-Off Broadway Explosion: How Provocative Playwrights of the 1960s Ignited a New American Theater*, David Crespy argues, as the title suggests, that the Off-Off Broadway theatre movement was the result of playwright initiation. Joe Cino, Reverend Al Carmine, and Edward Albee all had a hand in shaping Off-Off Broadway, which would lead to a larger turn for the American playwright. Crespy suggests that it is the "pioneer" spirit of the Off-Off Broadway artist that resulted in a proliferation of small theatre houses across the country (12-13):

> Off-Off Broadway stages are found thousands of miles from New York—in Seattle, Minneapolis, Austin, Chicago, Los Angeles—wherever there are artists hungry to produce fresh work. For emerging playwrights, Off-Off Broadway is a place to see their work performed without depending on producers, agents, directors, or other third-party endorsers. It's a theater that places primary focus on new scripts peopled with extraordinary characters telling powerful tales, using all the magical directorial and acting talents to bring it to life, even on the barest of stages and usually on a shoestring. It is a theatre where a poverty of means fuels an explosion of imagination—and it may happen anywhere in the country, anywhere in the world where theatre artists are determined to have a place of their own (13).

Having a place of one's own is an asset for any theatre artist. As theatre is a collaborative art, I argue, we who work in the theatre thrive by creating our own communities. Indeed, Crespy ends his book with suggestions on how to create your own Off-Off Broadway movement.

Playwright Jeffrey Sweet is no stranger to the pioneer spirit. As the initial Off-Off Broadway explosion was seeing its last glimmer in the 1970s, Sweet would be a founding member of The New York Writer's Bloc, a developmental workshop run by theatre folks without having the administrative restrictions of a theatre with a developmental wing. What made the Bloc unique was that it was created *by* playwrights: a do-it-yourself answer to some of the problems found in other developmental programs. Another factor that made it unique was the Bloc's invitation to actors and directors to join them. I believe that by looking back on the practices of non-funded, do-it-yourself organizations such as the Bloc, playwrights will become inspired to build their own development opportunities the way that playwrights have demonstrated the confidence to create their own production companies (which will be discussed in the next chapter).

Jeffrey Sweet was an emerging dramatic critic and non-academic historian. During his undergraduate work (he earned a Bachelor of Fine Arts in Film from New York University in 1971), Sweet was invited to the National Critics Institute at the O'Neill Conference in 1970 (although he has led workshops and seminars at the O'Neill Conference, Sweet has never had a play developed there). During the 1970s, Sweet wrote a number of shorter plays (including a musical), but spent the better portion of his time creating his book *Something Wonderful Right Away: An Oral History of the Second City and The Compass*. Sweet joined the Playwrights Unit at The Actors Studio in order to hone his craft as a dramatist, as he already had the training and inclination to be a theatre journalist.

The Playwrights Unit did not offer the experience Sweet had hoped for; rather, it set up a kind of competition among the playwrights, one that Sweet suggests is akin to a "Ben Hur chariot race" (Sweet Interview). Part of the issue was that Israel Horovitz, who ran the unit, was also "bringing in his own work" for review, "and if you had the temerity to criticize it frequently he would retaliate by shredding yours in turn" (Sweet, *The Dramatist's Toolkit*, 143). Michael Wright, who was a stage manager at the Actors Studio between 1977 and 1979, was having similar thoughts about the process:

> [I]f a given playwright's work didn't come off the page easily, it was immediately questioned as to whether it had any quality, and there wasn't any time spent on investigating what was going on with that particular set of pages. It either worked or it didn't. I thought that was too binary. I thought there was a huge middle ground they weren't exploring (Wright Interview).

The Actors Studio's Playwrights Unit continued the tradition of streamlining work to fit the single aesthetic of American Realism (character-driven, linear, cause-and-effect based, overtly emotional works) both by continuing to adhere to the notion that not all works had intrinsic worth (or were worthy of revision), and by giving only cursory attention to works that did not jump off the page on a first read. The aesthetic streamlining of the works, teamed up with the sense of competition that was spurred by the PU's director, Horovitz, led Sweet to decide to create a workshop that operated outside of the auspices of The Actors Studio. Wright, who had worked on a couple of scripts with Sweet at the Playwrights Unit, was approached to form a new group with Sweet.

Donald Margulies was another playwright looking for an artistic home. Like Sweet, he was also disappointed with developmental programs at that time. As an MFA in Creative Writing student at Brooklyn College, Margulies felt stifled: "Initially, I listened to feedback far too much. But what invariably happened in those early days is that I didn't find my play, I lost it; I lost sight of the play I was attempting to write" (30). Frustrated with the practices of developmental programs and dropping out of Brooklyn College, Margulies called his mentor at SUNY Purchase, Julius Novick, and asked if he could recommend an alternative:

> He [Novick] put me in touch with Jeffrey Sweet who, coincidentally, was in the process of organizing a writers' unit for the Encompass Theatre, a tiny Off-Off Broadway space on West 48th Street above a topless bar. It was in the fall of 1978 that the group that would come to be known as The New York Writers' Bloc came into existence (33).

The name "Writers' Bloc" is, of course, a pun. On the one hand, it suggests that writers sometimes get stuck, and thus need an environment in which to grow; on the other, "bloc" connotes a military coalition, a unified front. As Sweet recounts in *The Dramatist's Toolkit*, "When the group began, I wanted to call it Negotiating Stage[…] but Anne Meara, who was a member for several years, instantly said, 'That's the most pretentious fucking thing I've ever heard!' Someone else came up with the name the Writers' Bloc, and that stuck" (144).

It should be noted that Anne Meara, whom Sweet references, is an actor. Unlike the Playwrights Unit at the Actors Studio, the Bloc invited actors and directors to participate in exercises and the creation of scripts. This was a marked change from the ideology of the Playwrights Unit, where actors were brought in only if pieces were being presented in front of members. At the Playwrights Unit, the actors often read cold, and therefore any subtlety in the script would be lost. However, with the Bloc, actors were an essential and welcome component of the process. One of these actors was Jane Anderson, who suggests that the Bloc was invaluable for her as an actress, and ultimately, as a writer. Anderson remembers:

> I joined The Bloc, because […] when you're an actress, you're always looking for material to do. So, I thought 'oh, cool, I'll join this group and I'll meet playwrights and directors.' I was in the first play that put David [Mamet] on the map at the Cherry Lane Off-Broadway, but what I found most interesting in my experience in being in the play was the rehearsal process, and deconstructing David's words and getting to the subtext. And I found I was much more interested in the written experience than acting. And I think I suspected subconsciously that I was really meant to be a writer (Anderson Interview).

Word of mouth spread quickly about this new playwriting workshop that was open to actors and directors as well.

The New York Writers' Bloc began meeting in the fall of 1978 at Jane Anderson's one-bedroom apartment (Margulies, 33). Anderson notes, "My living room wasn't large by my living standards today, but back then we were all living in closet-sized spaces… About 10 or 20 of us would gather in my living room, and I'd have coffee and cookies, and we'd get to work" (Anderson Interview). Sweet remembers, "We were there a lot. But we bounced around a lot, as people's apartments opened up, somebody would say 'geez, this is a long commute for me, can we do a couple of them at my house?'" At one point, the Circle in the Square (uptown) offered the company a space, as a "community outreach thing" (Sweet Interview). The Bloc would continue to meet in New York until the mid-1980s (the date changes depending which Bloc member you speak with; Sweet has suggested the group met for ten years (Sweet Message); Jane Anderson has said that she continues a version of The Bloc in Los Angeles (Anderson email); there is also an unaffiliated reading series called The Writers' Bloc Play Festival in Chicago).

This look back at the creation of the New York Writers' Bloc provides an understanding of the perspectives of the writers, actors, and directors involved in the formation of the company: the playwrights were looking to create for themselves alternatives to the developmental programs that diminished their authority; some members were directors who had built relationships with playwrights; and some members, like Jane Anderson, were actors looking to make connections with writers. In short, these founding members were a company looking to create theatre in an environment that was nurturing, democratic, respectful, and constructive.

IMPROVISATION AND PLAYWRITING

The Bloc is distinct from other playwriting workshops due to Jeffrey Sweet's strong interest in improvisation. Perhaps his most recognized work is *Something Wonderful Right Away: An Oral History of the Second City and the Compass Players*. Throughout this book and most of Sweet's publications, there are generous nods to the improvisation techniques (often referred to as "theatre games") of teacher and improviser Viola Spolin and her son Paul Sills, who was the co-founder of Second City Chicago with Howard Alk and Bernie Sahlins. The Compass Players was led by Del Close, who created the "Harold," a long-form improvisation technique that builds an entire show (of skits and vignettes) based on an audience suggestion of a title or theme for the evening.

Viola Spolin was drawn to theatre, as well as the (improvised) games she had seen developed for new urban populations (geared to help immigrants adjust to big-city life). She believed improvisation was an excellent tool for education, and developed theatre games as a pedagogy. As a theatre director, Spolin did not "impose blocking and bits of business" on actors, but rather allowed the actors to find "solutions to dramatic problems [that] originated out of their own imaginations" via the "idea of playing games" (Sweet "The Innovators…"). In Spolin's words, from her book *Improvisation for the Theater*:

> The game is a natural group form providing the involvement and personal freedom necessary for experiencing. Games develop personal technique and skills necessary for the game itself, *through playing*. Skills are developed at the very moment a person is having all the fun and excitement playing a game has to offer— that is the exact time one is truly open to receive them [emphasis added] (4-5).

For Spolin, the participant in the exercise is learning her or his skill at the moment that he or she accepts the offer to play the game. In "Spolin and Sills Laid Down the Rules. The Generations Who Came After Played by Them. That's How Chicago Invented Itself," Todd London argues (as the rather lengthy title states) that the imaginative play fostered by Spolin and Sills created Chicago theatre, and in a way, created Chicago's Jewish identity:

> Each [theatre / improvisation] game centers on one aspect of imaginative reality: transforming space, fashioning objects out of air, creating a "where." The rules provide the player with a clear

focus or "point of concentration." By keeping their "eyes on the ball" and staying within the rules, the players free themselves to act spontaneously and creatively in the imaginary world. More-over, they learn to share space, to take impulses for action off of [sic] others, to give and take. [...] According to Sheldon Patinkin, artistic director of the National Jewish Theater in suburban Skokie and artistic consultant to Second City, the games "give the actors a sense of what it means to behave publicly as opposed to acting. And all you have to do is follow the rules" (London).

There are two points worth noting: one, community can be created via imaginative play. The second, theatre can also be created by accepting an offer from the Other, akin to one of Spolin's "sayings" found in the introduction of *Improvisation for the Theatre*: "Games and story bring out self rather than ego" (xv). Method-based acting relies on the ego and explorations of personal psychology in order to create an emotional need for a character, whereas improvisation relies on external forces—space, and most importantly, other people—to bring out a sense of self. As David Krasner suggests in "I Hate Strasberg," the introduction to *Method Acting Reconsidered: Theory, Practice, Future*:

> In Method acting [as practiced at The Actors Studio], actors are recognized as beings guided by their own intentions; in contrast, non-Method acting frequently views actors as subject to the imposition of external events. [...] The Method maintains that actors are free to perform and *control* actions and to determine their goals and objectives (17).

It should be noted that Krasner is actually defending Method-based acting, and the Method-actor's desire to *control* external circumstances in the service of fulfilling a character's emotional need. With improvisation, however, performers give over any sense of control, in order to build relationships via acting in co-operation with the other participants in the game. This is not to say that Method is without value—a number of Hollywood performers use Strasberg-based techniques in order to create the illusion of the first time when doing multiple takes. Furthermore, a number of actors use Method-based exercise to emotionally prepare for a character's first entrance in a performance. However, improvisation, especially when script building, allows the Other *in*, which can be quite a nerve-wracking process as the performer (and writer!) surrenders control.

For Sweet, this latter approach, one of playing games in order to create a theatre that involves an extension of an active-self, with actors working together in a codified and mutually created (imagined) space, became life-changing. As Sweet states, "Most of my ideas about the theoretical underpinnings of the theatre have their roots in [Spolin's] explorations" ("The Innovators...").

In "The Elements of Improvisation: Structural Tools for Spontaneous Theatre," Nicolas J. Zaunbrecher draws the dividing line between "improvisation as a category of actions" and "improvisation as a method for action" (49). Whereas the former involves spur-of-the-moment thinking in day-to-day life (which, for Zaunbrecher, includes actors ad-libbing if they forget their lines), the latter "method for action," is not a means of dealing with an unforeseen complication (in life or on stage), but rather "is deliberate and agreed-upon by its performers as a pre-given structure, not a fallback position enacted when a prescribed performance fails" (49). Furthermore, Zaunbrecher states that, with improvisational theatre, the performer's body (including voice) is itself the experienced site of performance content" (49). While it is commonplace to think of a body as a codified "text" in performance (see "Pastiche and Postmodern Playwriting"), the structured improvisational exercises used by the Bloc as a means of playwriting *pedagogy* suggest that a play-text should be a codebook for behavior; in other words, characters aren't just "saying"(dialogue), they are "doing" (action).

Although the environment of the Bloc was incredibly nurturing, the use of theatre games as a means of creating scripts and "solving problems" (a term Sweet uses when he is stuck with a particular scene) does not suggest that the writer was free to do what he or she liked without a set of guidelines or practices. As Zaunbrecher says:

> An easy rallying call for improv has long been that it is somehow "freer," or less limiting, than scripted theatre. This is misleading. The limitations work differently, and we should respect them for what they are, not try to pretend that they are less of a factor. Limitation in improv is not just a fact—it is essential and valuable (54).

By using an improvisational approach (i.e., theatre games), there is the suggestion that members of the Bloc were writing, more-or-less, a form of realism. However, unlike its Actors Studio counter-part, this playwriting workshop encouraged actors to write and writers to act in improvisational scenarios, allowing everyone to experience the body in motion, the subtleties of gesture, and the creation of *subtext* rather than on-the-nose-text. Furthermore, games allow writers to lose any notions of failure. Two of Spolin's sayings, as remembered by Paul Sills: "Approval/disapproval is keeping you from a direct experience," and "Success/failure is a side product of the approval/disapproval syndrome. Trying to succeed or giving into failure drains us" (Spolin, iii). With improvisation, success occurs when a participant is playing the game; skill as a writer is developed over time, while, to be blunt, having fun playing each game. Key to the success of this approach was the freedom for all artists involved to talk honestly about the works being presented. Jeff Sweet has suggested that Bloc members changed the shape of his play *The Value of Names:*

> I started working on *The Value of Names* as a four-character play— the two older men, the actress daughter of one of them, and her boyfriend. I brought in drafts of three scenes featuring the boyfriend and each time my colleagues in the Bloc said, "He's not interesting. The others are interesting. He seems to be there only so she has someone to explain things to." After three attempts at making a function come alive as a character, I surrendered.

The Value of Names is a three-character play. Without the Bloc, I would have written it as a four-character play, then I would have had the torturous experience of trying to remove one character. That would have been more than a little unpleasant. The Bloc saved me from that, kept me from wasting time, and might even have saved the play (Sweet Second message).

In this example, the playwright ultimately listened to his colleagues, and their advice improved the play. What makes this collaborative approach different from changes made to a script during sessions at the Playwrights Unit is the spirit in which the notes were given and received. Sweet's fellow theatre artists had no stake in the play—none of the actors were assigned to perform in a reading, and none of the writers were competing with Sweet. Rather, the script was nurtured (which does not suggest that it was handled gingerly) by the members of the Bloc in order to be the best possible presentation of the story Sweet wished to tell. *The Value of Names* premiered at the Actors Theatre of Louisville in 1983, and has received additional productions with actors such as Ed Asner, Jack Klugman, and Hector Elizondo (Sweet interview).

While the continued life of *The Value of Names* can certainly be pinned to the Bloc, a number of writers, actors, and directors were just cutting their teeth at Bloc meetings. In order to meet the needs of all members (from the seasoned writer to the novice), the Bloc used warm-up exercises to alleviate pressures of sharing work. One of the most intriguing improvisational writing exercises was the Six Line, which, according to Michael Wright, "encouraged everyone to write just for the hell of it" (Email). Wright remembers:

> After we had met for about a year, some of us non-writers began to want to try some writing without having to go through the horrors of a critique. This was when the six-line was introduced (*Process*, 15).

The hope for Sweet was to get "the non-writers in the group to start writing" (Sweet Email to the playwrightbinge—an online community of playwrights). The Bloc was given an assigned topic, and each member—writer or not—would bring in six lines, "three pairs of exchanges between two people," based on the topic (Sweet Email to playwrightbinge). Sweet suggests, "almost nobody was too timid to write six lines," and furthermore, based on the confidence to *play* with writing, and "empowered by the success of six lines, actors indeed became writers" (Sweet email to the playwrightbinge). Donald Margulies also appreciated the Six Line, as "everyone is represented each week, with 'appetizers' that are short and sweet" (28). For Margulies, this foregrounded The Bloc's dedication to building a community:

> I learned in the Bloc the importance of feeding the investment of a group through the work of the individuals. Six Lines seemed to do that; everyone looked forward to hearing not only their own efforts but those of their colleagues as well. We would come up with a single word or phrase—"First Love" comes to mind—and

everyone would write his or her six exchanges of dialogue based on that phrase. Some of my early efforts grew out of these explorations (28-29).

A theatre game offers participants the freedom to explore and discover (as an individual), while maintaining fidelity to the guiding framework of the particular game (within the community). In other words, The Bloc, a playwright-centered workshop, not only focused on creating new work, it also foregrounded notions of theatricality and community.

THEATRICALITY AND COMMUNITY

For Michael Wright, to work *theatrically* is to recognize a script as one component of production (*Process*, 15). This idea of working theatrically was a new addition to the workshop model, creating the sense that the writer was not working in a literary vacuum, but creating something that had three dimensions via collaboration with actors and directors during the early stages of development. Furthermore, actors and directors would learn the craft of the writer, in order to fully engage in a common vocabulary. The common vocabulary, or theatrical language, would lead to the development of the Bloc-as-community.

The Bloc met for three to four hours per session, but as members became more invested in one another's lives, they would spend an additional two to three hours to get coffee, talk, and socialize. This social aspect was an important component to Bloc meetings because, as Sweet notes, a playwright "need[s] to have a community base or you feel like a lone gunslinger. With very few bullets" (Sweet Interview). Donald Margulies remembers:

> In the beginning, Jeffrey [Sweet], as the organizer of the group, set the tone of our discourse and did a remarkable job of bringing people together. But as the group matured, it outgrew the single-moderator format and, in order to survive and flourish, adopted a rotating system so that from week to week a different member of the core group was responsible for moderating critiques (34).

Giving each member the opportunity to lead discussion helped steer the participants toward an artistic democracy, a step away from the sense of competition-with-the-moderator fostered (whether intentional or not) at the Playwrights Unit. Sweet, who at first was the sole moderator, suggests that members of the Bloc were taught how to critique one another's work, a skill that had been (and still is) lacking in new play development sessions. Anderson describes:

> Jeff's rule was that when you critiqued each other's work, you never say what *you* would write, you would always try to ask what the writer wanted to convey, and let them know if they succeeded with that. And that formula was what makes these kinds of

groups so successful. I've taken part in workshops that have been sponsored by theatres, with a formal dramaturge and with some people offering criticism, and I've often found that workshops are more destructive than helpful because it makes the playwright go in all kinds of directions that he or she never wanted to go in order to please the opinions of directors. There was a period of that at the Writer's Bloc (Interview).

In other words, the New York Writers' Bloc, as a playwriting workshop geared toward the writer rather than the play, focused on the individual writer's craft, building a life-long confidence for members, while creating networking opportunities among the various actors, directors, and designers who participated. This Feast of St. Crispianesque "band of friends" created for themselves a nurturing environment, which not only suited their needs, but pushed their boundaries as writers and theatre artists.

Although the Bloc was not a producing organization, it provided a comfortable arena for writers to experiment, hone their craft, and, though this may sound callow, have fun. When reflecting on the Bloc, Sweet says:

> Here's the kicker: it was run with no grants, no funding, no larger sheltering organization. It survived entirely on the most minuscule of dues—a couple of bucks a month per person to cover the cost of coffee and pastries. If the Bloc proves anything, it is that you don't need much to begin and sustain a vibrant and productive workshop. All that is necessary is a handful of idealistic, committed individuals and a living room big enough to hold them and their enthusiasm" (148).

While there was no set manifesto, Susan Merson recounts some of the (spoken and unspoken) rules for the Bloc: "Kindness and support brings talent forth more often than criticism," "Ignoring flaws in a writer's work consistently creates blockages for the writer and ennui in the group," "The more intimately the work was understood by the Bloc, the more helpful the comments for the writer" ("Teaching Philosophy"). While several developmental groups have used the term "support," this is the first time that the mission statement of a theatre group, however informal, included the terms "kindness" and "understanding" vis-à-vis the individual writer's process and the work he or she shares with the group. The notions of kindness and understanding operate in sharp contrast to the sense of competition—the "Ben Hur chariot race" atmosphere—found at the Playwrights Unit (Sweet interview).

But how does kindness aid a writer? Part of nurturing in the process of creating art is allowing others to make mistakes, and a willingness to make mistakes oneself. With the Bloc, an artist is making mistakes in front of other people. However, unlike other developmental programs, the Bloc encourages members to learn from their mistakes in an environment that gives everyone permission to fail. As David Cohen, an adjunct professor of Theatre Arts at SUNY New Paltz once said to me, "If you're not failing at least fifty percent of the time, you're not improvising."

Most important, the Bloc created a community, echoing the hopes of Viola Spolin and Paul Sills. As Todd London says of Paul Sills: "the idea of community supersedes the urge to make theatre. He considers his work 'para-theatrical'" ("Spolin"). London continues:

> In Sweet's chock-full oral history of the Compass and Second City, *Something Wonderful Right Away*, Sills quotes his favorite philosopher, Martin Buber, to explain: "The heavenly bread of self-being is passed between man and man." This interaction is possible in the "freespace" created by the games. Former Sills-protégé Patinkin puts it another way: "When you drop all the life problems and just invest yourself in solving problems within the rules of the game—and since the rules are always about getting what happens next off the person that you're responding to—it creates a sense of community" (London, "Spolin").

With Spolin's games, there were no winners or losers (that is, no competition). There was a community trying to figure out approaches to the problems of everyday life by creating scenes together; someone would create an imagined environment. Someone else would enter the imagined environment. The imagination operates as an invitation to the other to coexist in the game, and work together to solve a problem. Unlike the Stanislavski system or Method acting, the player in the scene has to work outside of her- or himself by sustaining the imagined world, and by trusting, reacting, and listening to the other player. The idea of listening to another, to truly engage with an "other" human being, is a valuable practice for both the art of playwriting and the art of building a community.

CONCLUSION FOR PLAYWRIGHT-CENTERED WORKSHOPS

(OR, CONTINUING THE PIONEER SPIRIT)

While the most immediate mark of playwright success is a production, there are successes located with playwriting workshops which are geared toward the writer, and that give the writer the artistic safety of communal bonds. Writers can build their own development opportunities by embracing the pioneer spirit of the Off-Off Broadway movement, and the artists-as-community spirit fostered by The New York Writers' Bloc. There are a number of excellent companies entirely run by playwrights (some with more visibility than others). Since the pioneering work of the Writers' Bloc, playwrights are increasingly taking leadership roles in the means of theatrical production, creating their own development opportunities, and welcoming writers as well as directors and actors in the spirit of camaraderie and improvisation.

CHAPTER *nine*

SCRIPT-CENTERED WORKSHOP

The roles of the script-centered workshop are essentially the same as the writer-centered workshop: you have the artist who brings the work, the responders who are engaged in a dialogue with the work, and the facilitator/moderator who creates the framing questions and guidelines for the evening. It differs insofar as you will be focusing on a single script by a single author, rather than short scenes by a group of writers. Script-Centered workshops are often offered by the developmental wing of an established theatre company. The scripts that are read are often (but not always) considered for production. Sometimes, the writer is a resident at the theatre company and they want to hear a work they've been developing. In the case of Rose of Athens reading series, the plays are read for the benefit of the writer as well as the community—we are teaching our audiences how to receive new plays (as the season consists mostly of family-friendly material, and summer outdoor Shakespeare productions). It is our hope to produce some of these plays in the near future.

HOW TO CREATE A
SCRIPT-CENTERED WORKSHOP

I was very fortunate. I arrived in Athens, Georgia and I met with Rose of Athens artistic director Lisa Cesnik Ferguson who had been hoping to create a new play reading series for her company. I had the same goal and we have made it work! The playwrights we feature include UGA students and alumni (including the New York Innovative Theatre Award-nominated Angela Hall and Tennessee Williams One Act Play Contest—Winner George Pate), community members, regional playwrights (from Atlanta and other parts of Georgia, including President of Working Title Playwrights Hank Kimmel and the Atlanta regional representative for The Dramatists Guild, Pamela Turner), and playwrights who have the ability to travel to Athens to hear one of their works read (including Ron Pullins of Massachusetts, Donna Latham of Ohio, and EJC Calvert and Dusty Wilson of Chicago, who all had to fly in to hear their plays!). Originally, our readings were held at Hendershots Coffee Bar in Athens, GA, and we later moved to the Studio Academy Dance Space. What I have learned is that you can have a play reading just about anywhere as long as folks can find it. Social media has made it possible to spread the word about each reading.

I do not charge admissions for readings. The readers are not paid. The playwrights who created the work are not paid. If you decide to charge admission, make sure you discuss this with the playwright and that he or she earns her fair share (and for this, you may want to consult the Dramatists Guild's business affairs office; I'm going to take it for granted that if you make it this far, you are a Guild member!). I always bring donuts, plates, napkins, and bottled water. Remember—most people will sit through anything for a free donut.

I tend not to rehearse the actors for the reading. We are currently operating under the auspices of No Shame, and even though I've broken most of the No Shame rules, the "no rehearsals" is something I have stuck to. Part of that is pure logistics: if you tell potential readers that there are no rehearsals, chances are they can free themselves up for an evening. If you plan on holding rehearsals, it might be a challenge to attract quality readers depending on your region. (Some towns are very theatre-friendly, some aren't. Keep this in mind as you move forward.)

The facilitator/moderator's role has not changed, however the responders might not be the same people who attend your writer-center workshop. Hopefully, you will attract a number of eager community members who love the theatre, but who might not have the vocabulary necessary for a constructive feedback session.[1] Probably the best run feedback session I've seen was at the Hollins Playwrights Festival, in which moderator Todd Ristau asked responders: "What resonated with you?" "What questions did the play leave you with?" and "Where did your attention drop?" These questions are not too different from Lerman's. Finally, Ristau turns to the playwright and asks if he or she has any questions for the responders. The playwright otherwise does not respond, other than to say, "thank you" for each note.

---

1 For an excellent look at audience talk-backs, see Teresa A. Fisher's *Post-Show Discussions in New Play Development.*

Two points: one, always have a set of questions ready, even if you decide not to use any of the above. Never, NEVER ask something as general as "what did you think?" Often, a well-meaning responder will hijack the conversation and attempt to rewrite the play in a way that he or she feels is more "suitable" (whatever that means). I have seen this happen far too many times. It would be better not to have a feedback session at all than to go into one without a plan. The second point: can a playwright speak? I don't have a hard, fast rule about this. Some organizations do. I often find it rewarding when the playwright has the opportunity to enter into a discussion with the responders. However, there are some playwrights who do get a bit defensive about their work, and this can result in a fruitless (and terribly frustrating, terribly long) conversation. The short answer: it's up to you! Just make sure you have a plan, and if you decide to allow the playwright to respond to questions, be ready for the answers.

Steps:
1. Find a space.
2. Find someone who can contribute to the cost of copies.
3. Find local writers who have scripts.
4. Bring donuts and water.

FIND A SPACE

For the script-centered workshop, talk to local coffee shops, book stores, libraries, and dance centers; you may even want to approach local schools to see if they would be willing to allow your reading in their auditorium (just clearly mark whether or not the play is intended for younger audiences). If you are fortunate enough to earn a space with a local theatre, you may want to ask if they would be willing to lend their name as well as their space. If you are lucky enough to live in an arts/theatre-friendly city, talk to art centers, theatre centers, etc., and see if they would be willing to host your reading. My motto is "you can't beat the price of free," however, if you do need to rent a space, make sure that you advertise the reading to reach the largest number of people. Visibility is key.

FIND SOMEONE WHO CAN CONTRIBUTE TO THE COST OF COPIES

If you do end up earning sponsorship from an arts center or a theatre company, then the cost of your copies should be covered. If not, there is nothing wrong with passing the hat after the reading and asking for donations to offset the cost of scripts. For less formal readings, the donations go toward the cost of copies and refreshments. For more formal readings, donations might help offset the cost of the space. In any case, people want to know where their money is going. You must let them know. Make your announcement after the reading, and send around the hat.

FIND LOCAL WRITERS WHO HAVE SCRIPTS

Always start locally; this helps ensure that writers will attend their readings. If you're doing a series, don't forget why you started this in the first place! *Make sure you have a slot for your own work.*

BRING DONUTS AND WATER

It's amazing what folks will sit through with the promise of free food!

As suggested, steps one and two can be accomplished by approaching a local theatre company to see if they would be interested in hosting your reading series. Make sure you approach the company with a plan. Start small: suggest one reading a month, or one every other month. Let them know what your goals are for the series (audience engagement above anything else), and how the series can help the theatre support the local community. When you do approach a company, make sure you don't come out with guns a-blazing. Shoot a quick email and wait for a reply. If you don't get one, try with another company. Better yet, call the literary manager from the local theatre to see if they would be interested in talking with you. If they are, wonderful! If not, try somewhere else. Worst case scenario: do it yourself. If you and members of your writer-centered community have a bunch of completed plays, throw some money in a hat and host your own reading series. This is a wonderful way to let the community know what you are up to and how you are hoping to serve them.

LAST FRONTIER THEATRE CONFERENCE: A CASE STUDY

The O'Neill Playwrights Conference is perhaps the most visible of the playwriting workshops, standing as both the inheritor of the historical tradition and the present-day status quo. Playwright Michael Wright has given an historical account of the O'Neill, locating three phases between its inception in 1968 and 2004 (Wright, *Playwriting at Work*). The center was first used by director Jose Quintero who did "experimentation with process that were the foundation for what eventually became the O'Neill approach" in 1965, however the O'Neill Conference did not begin formally until the leadership of Lloyd Richards in 1968 (25). This marks the first phase of the O'Neill, which ended when Richards resigned in 1999 (25-33). This phase was followed by the leadership of James Houghton (1999-2003), and then came the third phase, which involves two artistic directors, and the re-evaluation of the role of the O'Neill Playwrights Conference. Although The O'Neill Conference remains one of the most visible script-centered playwriting workshops, it has its detractors, who claim that the selection process has been rigged (Bray, "Process as Product," "What's Wrong with this Play;" Tec, "Open Submission"). Because The O'Neill conversation is a dividing factor among mid-career and seasoned playwrights, I would rather focus on The Last Frontier Theatre Conference (LFTC), a script-centered workshop run by playwright Dawson Moore.

Founded in 1992 and revamped in 2005,[2] LFTC borrows from the O'Neill Conference model insofar as playwrights are invited for a week-long residency in order to hear one of their plays. The LFTC creates an *imagined temporary community*. I am adapting Benedict Anderson's notion of an imagined community (in which nations are developed via print and literacy practices) and temporary communities (from experiential education studies), in order to create a material hybrid. With a temporary community, there is an emphasis on "the short-term, sharply delineated duration of residential camps and the sense of community that can result even in a relatively brief time" (Smith, Steel, and Gidlow, 137). For LFTC, that period of time is seven days. "Temporary communities are not only defined by its time frame[s]; [they] also provides an entirely different physical setting in which to interact" (137). For most of the LFTC participants, the location of Valdez, Alaska is far from a continental U.S. home. In addition, Alaska residents can only reach Valdez via a tiny airline from Anchorage (in which one does not have to pass through security), a treacherous nine-hour drive around icy and glacier-laden mountains, or a long boat ride from the coast near Anchorage. In other words, traveling to Valdez, Alaska already feels like a journey to the last frontier. Although still U.S. soil, there are geographic barriers to the rest of the continent, as well as the rest of Alaska itself, which cause the participant to feel that they are participating in another realm.

Valdez, Alaska is haunted both by the Exxon-Valdez oil spill in 1992, as well as by the late 19th century gold rush;[3] with the latter, the town self-consciously has preserved its gold-rush-era vernacular. The buildings are aesthetically similar, and some feature murals of men looking for gold in the icy waters. The result is that travelers are meant to feel that they are traveling to another time, locked in the hope for prosperity (gold) and the potential disasters in mining the earth (Exxon Valdez).

LFTC itself also operates differently than other workshops. As Dawson Moore suggests, LFTC does not offer a playwright a director (which more popular conferences, such as the O'Neill, generally do); also, there is only one rehearsal prior to a reading of a playwright's play. However, Moore contends:

> ...it's hard for me to imagine a much more enriching overall experience for a playwright than the week they spend with us in Valdez. The greatest challenge of our event, the number of playwrights we endeavor to serve each year, is also the source of our greatest asset: community. Each year, we create a collaboration between over 200 artists for a week, with around a fourth of those being writers. They range from highly trained professionals to first time writers, and we create a non-competitive environment for them to interact (Moore, Message to the Author).

---

2 Founder Dr. Jo Ann C. McDowell would leave Valdez in 2005, and create the Great Plains Theatre Conference in the midwest. At this time, playwright Dawson Moore restructured the LFTC to place the emphasis on "early and mid-career" playwrights/Play Labs participants, rather than build an event around a single featured known playwright/respondent. For a full history, see: http://www.theatreconference.org/about/conference-history/

3 It should be noted that Exxon is a major contributor to LFTC, as it has worked for the past 20 years to improve its public image and forge stronger community connections.

At the LFTC, playwrights are not put in competition with one another. They are not there to serve an author, to serve an academic discipline, or to serve the necessities of attracting grants (though, this is certainly a byproduct). Rather, the playwrights are invited to partake in, and build, a temporary community, and any sense of playwriting hierarchy is removed (i.e., accepted writers include seasoned professionals and beginners) in the spirit of generosity.

With imagined temporary communities, there are performed activities that mark participants as members. With LFTC, the activities include a reading of one's own play, as well as a "monologue slam," an evening performance each of the seven nights, improvisational troupes, and the ability to participate in a late night Fringe Festival. For actors, there are monologue and vocal workshops. Additionally, LFTC hosts a glacier tour and a final banquet. The town is small enough in population (4,032 in 2011) that one of the local bars opens every night for karaoke. As Moore suggests:

> All of these things, coupled with a stimulating dramaturgical environment, create a week-long overall experience designed to strengthen one's knowledge and enrich their souls. Some people come once and get what they need; some come every two to four years to recharge their battery; and some attend every year as a mandatory part of their artistic life. Every year, numerous collaborations are birthed from the friendships that are formed here (Moore Message).

The enriching of the playwright's soul takes place with the building of, and participation in, the imagined temporary community. The playwrights, mostly outsiders to Valdez, are brought together to form their own bonds by staying in residential dorms, participating in karaoke, and exploring Valdez wildlife, as if on vacation or away at camp. The distance one travels, as well as the preserved gold rush vernacular, and even the very name "Last Frontier" suggests an otherworld, a place in which participants will be welcomed to form their own communities outside of the realm of the real. However, as Moore suggests, the bonds formed have continued past the LFTC, as a number of artists continue to work with one another.[4]

When you create your script-centered workshop, your goal should be to engage with your community. You may want to create a week-long festival of readings, or have readings of new scripts on a monthly basis (or four times a year; really, the number of plays is up to you). When you make the commitment to create a reading series, you are not only creating a valuable opportunity for writers (including yourself), you are also teaching your local community how to be an audience for new work.

---

4 For example, the Full Circle Theatre Company in downtown NYC has produced several evenings of one-act plays written by past LFTC Play Labs participants. The company is led by LFTC alumni Nicholas Herbert.

WORKSHOP PRODUCTION?

In 2011, I sat next to one of my favorite playwrights during a cue-to-cue of a workshop production of his play. The workshop production would run for three nights with no audience talk-back. It was a very bizarre experience. The actors were almost entirely off-book. At one point, the writer leaned over to me and asked, "Why won't they just call it a production?" I think this is a very important question, as most indie theatre productions are fairly minimalistic due to having a smaller budget. However, established theatres with a larger budget may be hesitant to fully mount a new work due to the financial risk involved.

So, what is a workshop production? Perhaps the best working definition comes from Leroy Clark's *Writing for the Stage: a Practical Playwriting Guide*:

> A workshop production is a very low-budget affair. Its purpose is to mount a production of the play with actors who are fully committed to the roles and perform the play in front of an audience and see how it works. During the rehearsal process, the playwright is able to do some rewriting and tweak the script here and there to improve it. The production values—sets, costumes, lighting, sound, and props—are minimal. Sometimes, the show is done in front of black drapes with stock furniture and props and basic lighting (261).

There are a couple of important suggestions in this definition. The first is the description "*very* low-budget [emphasis added]," as it suggests minimal risk. If a small amount of money is put into a work, then the theatre may only charge a donation, or a much lower ticket price (if tickets are offered; some workshop productions offer a front-and-back photocopied program in lieu of a ticket and fully-realized program). The other suggestion is that a work is not complete, as a playwright can perform "rewrites," and "tweak"-ing in order to "improve" the script (by whatever standards the theatre company feels the script needs improvement). Based on interviews with several playwrights, I can confirm that the tweaking of a script used to happen during the rehearsal process geared toward production (in particular, Jeffrey Sweet, Michael Wright, and Bob Jude Ferrante, raised this point). With the rise of developmental programs, reworking a script now occurs during developmental workshops, rather than rehearsals.

There are other concerns that emerge as well: by pairing the words "workshop" and "production," the workshop becomes a *surrogate* for an actual production. The process, as I have argued elsewhere, is the product. The workshop production becomes the pinnacle of playwright success, creating further distance between emerging (as well as seasoned) writers and the opportunity to have a work fully mounted. Furthermore, because the workshop is a production, the expectations are created that the work is still in need of "fine tuning," and, therefore, is not complete. The playwright assumes the position, consciously or not, of someone who needs further help with the work, and his or her own craft.

Another issue with the rise of the workshop and the workshop production is the role of rehearsal for a fully-mounted production. That is, the workshop production stands in for a full production, and the readings that lead up to a workshop production stand in for the rehearsal process. In a phone interview, Roland Tec, the Director of Membership for the Dramatists Guild of America, suggested that the workshop process has created an aesthetic that removes a sense of theatricality from the written word:

> One of the dangers is that people start writing for readings. And the kind of writing that works well with a sit down reading is not the same kind of writing that works well with putting something on its feet. And I think we're in danger of writing things that are in a very narrow kind of language (Tec Interview).

Tec highlights the problems of writing for readings, echoing the concerns of a number of playwrights (see *Outrageous Fortune* and Teresa A. Fisher's *Post-Show Discussions in New Play Development*). One way to help ease these concerns is to lay out very specific goals with the artistic team for the reading, workshop, or workshop production. For the reading, the goal could be simply to hear the dialogue. For the closed workshop, the director and actors should be working through the moment-to-moment of the script, and/or a plan for the aesthetic experience. Furthermore, there must be an agreement that if the play is moving to the workshop production phase, all involved must be ready to commit to a full production.

These are issues to keep in mind as you move forward with developing your own opportunities and while participating in opportunities with established theatre organizations. All parties involved are usually quite good natured, but it is easy to fall into established habits of development as a surrogate for production. This is why it is more important than ever for you to take artistic control of your piece from development through the fully realized production.

CONCLUSION

You, as playwright, are engaging with the pioneer spirit. When you start a developmental program, you are not just engaging with an audience via your letter to the world, you are building a community of artists and audiences. Whether you create a program in which a play is read once every other month or a week-long festival, you are helping to shape the American theatre by creating shared, imagined community. Your program just might incite others to start writing plays, which is a very rewarding experience.

CHAPTER *ten*

CREATING YOUR OWN PRODUCTION OPPORTUNITIES

PRODUCING YOUR OWN WORK

In the summer of 2014, I was a guest respondent for the Hollins Play Labs Playwrights Festival at the Mill Mountain Theatre in Roanoke, Virginia. The program coordinator is Todd Ristau, a playwright who founded the No Shame movement on the back of his pickup truck in 1986. (No Shame is an evening of theatre/performance in which folks sign up and present a five-minute work that has never been rehearsed; there are now dozens of No Shames around the country, each hosted by a different theatre or performance organization.) The other guest respondents included such luminaries as Robert Moss, founder of Playwrights Horizon and former artistic director of Edward Albee's Playwrights' Unit; Jane B. Jones, Education Manager at Actors Theatre of Louisville; Mary Harvey Levine, a well-produced playwright; James Merchant, program coordinator for the Arts Administration undergraduate degree at Elon University; and Gwydion Suilebhan, the DC representative for The Dramatists' Guild of America, Inc. and a founding member of The Welders, a playwrights collective (I should note that there were 25 respondents in all, each with exciting theatre world experience). During one of our dinners together, Suilebhan informed us that according to his research (published on HowlRound, the official blog for Arena Stage, and elsewhere), there are 15,000 self-identified playwrights living in the U.S., and each year only 1,500 production opportunities. That means there are only 10% of us getting our work produced each year. Because of this alarming number, playwrights have turned to self-producing.

The July/August 2009 issue of *The Dramatists*, the official journal for The Dramatists' Guild of America, Inc., was dedicated to playwrights who also act as self-producers. Self-production, many have argued, is a vital next step as production opportunities are becoming more limited. Lisa Soland of Granada Hills, California argues:

> What will happen is that in a very short amount of time, you'll realize that this [being a producer] is very doable and you will start to lose the idea that your writing career is at the mercy of someone else; someone other than yourself. Your entire nature will change and you will gain strength in your self-reliance (9).

In other words, Soland believes that "self-reliance" in the mechanism of production builds confidence, both as a writer and as a collaborator. Furthermore, I argue that the craft of playwriting is only truly learned when the playwright sees his or her own work in production.

Producing your own work can be a fairly daunting task, but it is most emphatically not impossible. After you have had the chance to do it a few times, it will get easier. Self-producing will also impact your writing, as you will consider creative ways in your script to solve problems that may emerge in a full production. The first step is to make sure you have a play that you feel is ready (or, ready enough) for production. Even if you take your play through a series of workshops, knowing when a work is ready is something you have to intuit. One person in your workshop might feel it is ready, someone else might feel it isn't. Only you can be the final judge. The steps to self-producing look a little like finding a space for a reading.

Steps:
1. Have a goal.
2. Find a space.
3. Create an *honest* budget.
4. Consider fiscal sponsorship.
5. Fundraise.
6. Act as artistic director.

YOUR GOAL?

Granted, your goal is to produce your play, but where do you want to see it staged? How long do you imagine the run? One week? Two weeks? Three? How many nights per week? Will you have a Sunday matinee? (When I lived in

Louisiana, I self-produced a fairly gory play. I opted not to have a Sunday matinee because I knew that the matinee crowds tended to be folks coming from church. I did not want to give the impression that the play was family friendly. This might not have been a concern of mine if I had produced the play in downtown, NYC. Know your region!)

FIND A SPACE

If you want to stage your play in a traditional theatre space, start looking! If you're in a theatre-friendly city like Manhattan, you can easily research what spaces are available, but just a heads up: as the number of independent theatre spaces has diminished, the price of rental has significantly increased. In 1999, a self-producing playwright could rent a 99-seat-or-under theatre space for roughly $5,000 for the run. Now, the rent would be closer to $15,000. If you wish to use union actors, your cost becomes much higher (see Playwrights Collectives for a discussion about the Basic Showcase Contract). If you are living in an area where there are theater spaces, whether community theatres, or theatres operating under smaller equity contracts, you can ask them about the possibility of rental. Some places might say no (due to union regulations or otherwise), but don't get discouraged. Make a list of where you would most like to see your play, followed by the second most, followed by the third, etc. Go down your list. You will find someplace, but it may require you to think outside of the box.

If it turns out there aren't any traditional theatre spaces available to you (or, if you're living in an area where there aren't many theatre spaces), investigate some non-theatrical spaces, such as art galleries, dance studio spaces, coffee houses, and gymnasiums. In Chicago, there are a number of store-front theatre companies. In fact, one of the best productions of my play, *Goodnight Lovin' Trail*, went up in a storefront as part of the Delaware Fringe Festival in Wilmington. The play is set in a diner. The venue directors had suggested we have the action take place toward the back of the venue, and they would black out the windows. Instead, director Akia Squitieri decided to use the windows and functional door as the set. It's a diner, after all! As folks walked by on the street, they became part of the set, and part of the audience's experience. The result was amazing! Playwright Mariah MacCarthy produced her play (with her company Caps Lock Theatre), *The Foreplay Play*, at a friend's apartment! As MacCarthy notes, "The last non-festival, 12-performance production of a play of mine was done at The Paradise Factory, a gorgeous but modest black box space on East 4th Street. The Paradise Factory rents for $2,500/week. The entire budget for the 12-performance run of *The Foreplay Play* was $3,000. The *entire* budget" (MacCarthy). She is addressing a very practical concern—the budget! MacCarthy split the box office with the apartment tenants, and the play went on to earn two New York Innovative Theatre Award nominations (the NYITs are the Tony's of the Off-Off Broadway/New York Indie Theatre world).[1] The key concern is to find a space. Remember, theatre is an abstract medium and can happen anywhere. Do not limit your imagination.

---

1 For more on MacCarthy's experiences, please visit New York Theatre Reviews essays on using non-theatrical spaces. MacCarthy's entry can be read here: http://newyorktheatrereview.blogspot.com/2012/05/reinventing-play-series-of-essays-on.html

You will also need a space for your rehearsals. In college and high school, we get spoiled: there is always some space available for us to rehearse. Many times, we are able to use the actual theatre for most of our rehearsals. This rarely ever happens outside of academic and community theatre settings. Rehearsal space can be just as challenging to find as a space for the production. If you live in NYC, there are a number of spaces available through ART/NY, as well as spaces via cultural centers, galleries, theatres, dance studios, etc. Keep in mind that these places will charge a fee, and the rates are regularly increasing (in 2009 I rented a dance studio for $20 an hour and considered myself lucky). You may want to think about having your rehearsals at your apartment, at public parks (just be mindful that other folks might not want to hear you rehearse); really, any place that's free.

For those of us who live outside of NYC: you can hold your early rehearsals at apartments, houses, and public spaces (again, being mindful of anyone who might not want to hear you rehearse); some coffee houses have a back room; some high schools and colleges may be willing to let you use a space; the bottom line is you need to ask. This will take some legwork. The earliest rehearsals, which will probably be table reads, can be held just about anywhere. Once the actors start moving around, it can be a bit more difficult to find a space that meets your needs. Ask—ask early, ask often.

CREATE AN *HONEST* BUDGET AND CONSIDER FISCAL SPONSORSHIP

I'm bringing these two items together for this section. Your budget and fiscal sponsorship consideration need to happen at virtually the same time. Use a spreadsheet to create a line by line item. I would suggest making two budgets: one would be your dream budget, and the second would be the bare minimum of what you would need in order to make the play happen (although, playwright Edward Albee once quipped, ""I've always thought that any play that can't be done with two chairs and a light bulb has problems") (McAlister).

Below is an example of a budget plan created by Jerrod Bogard for one of my plays. Early in the process, we were going to co-produce the work in one of the New York theatre festivals. I am happy to say that the Rising Sun Performance Company, an Off-Off Broadway theatre troupe, has agreed to give the play its world premiere with Bogard directing. (At the time of writing this, dates and locations are TBA. I am sure by the time this book is published, the show will have already had its run.)

When Bogard and I originally decided to co-produce the work in a festival, we came up with three budgets, the first being our day dream, the second being ideal, and the third being the lowest amount we would need to have a successful run of the show. I have included the spreadsheet on the following page. Notice that we decided not to use union actors for the show, which means we would not have to secure any basic showcase codes; however, most festivals still require independent producers to purchase insurance. We also decided that all artists involved should be given a stipend for their time. (Although, with the third budget, I waived my fee; keep in mind that many playwrights would disapprove of the idea of not getting paid for their work. It is a hot issue in the playwriting community. The decision is ultimately very personal).

Budget estimate Play: ERIK				
EXPENSE	**COST plan 1**	**COST plan 2**	**COST plan 3**	**NOTES**
Fringe Fee	$600.00	$600.00	$600.00	
Venue Director	$150.00	$150.00	$150.00	
Insurance	$300.00	$300.00	$300.00	
Set materials	$500.00	$400.00	$300.00	
Costumes	$400.00	$350.00	$300.00	remainder is stipend to costumer
Puppets	$500.00	$400.00	$300.00	
Props	$200.00	$150.00	$100.00	
Light Design	$100.00	$50.00	$0.00	I can design lights for rep plot
Set Design	$200.00	$100.00	$75.00	includes construction stipend
Costume Design	$200.00	$150.00	$75.00	includes construction stipend
Sound Design	$100.00	$50.00	$0.00	includes show operation
Actors	7 x $200	7 x $100	7 x $50	Non-Union- "Favored Nations"
	$1,400.00	$700.00	$350.00	
Puppeteers	2 x $200	2 x $100	2 x $50	Non-Union- "Favored Nations"
	$400.00	$200.00	$100.00	
Stage Manager	$300.00	$250.00	$200.00	
Director	$400.00	$350.00	$300.00	
Playwright	$250.00	$125.00	$0.00	
Rehearsal	$1,000.00	$1,000.00	$800.00	
Postcards	$150.00	$125.00	$125.00	
Adds	$600.00	$400.00	$300.00	
Press Representat.	$1,500.00	$1,000.00	$0.00	
Truck/Car rental	$150.00	$100.00	$100.00	
Miscelani	$200.00	$200.00	$200.00	
TOTAL	$9,600.00	$7,150.00	$4,675.00	

Seeing the numbers can help you see how "do-able" your show is, and also give you a clear idea of how much work you'll need to put into your play. Another piece of valuable advice (taking a page from Mel Brooks' *The Producers*): never use your own money to fund a show. I will return to this point in just a moment.

Depending on the size of your production, you may want to consider finding fiscal sponsorship with an agency such as Fractured Atlas. These organizations are extraordinarily helpful. First of all, it means you do not have to create a non-profit company. By having a fiscal sponsor, donations may become tax-deductible (you will have to talk with someone at one of these organizations for a specific plan). Furthermore, Fractured Atlas provides liability insurance, which is very important. Be sure to research Fractured Atlas and The Field before you begin any fundraising.

FUNDRAISING: HOW TO NOT USE YOUR OWN MONEY

When you produce a show, you should never use your own money. You will go broke pretty quickly. As most theatre is nonprofit, there is a very slim chance of actually earning a living. The best you can hope for is breaking even. This is an unfortunate economic reality. Is this how it should be? Certainly not! What we do is incredibly hard work and we should have a right to a living wage. Unfortunately, that's simply not the case. Not right now, anyway. While I could editorialize on the terrible treatment artists receive in the U.S., I'd rather talk to you about crowdsourcing.

According to the *Merriam-Webster Dictionary*, crowdsourcing is defined as "the practice of obtaining needed services, ideas, or content by soliciting contributions from a large group of people and especially from the online community rather than from traditional employees or suppliers" (*Merriam-Webster* online). For our purposes, crowdsourcing is the soliciting of monetary donations for your production using the Internet. You can crowdsource by posting messages on social media with links to donation pages, or you can use sites such as Kickstarter and Indiegogo to give your project visibility beyond your network of friends. Many mainstream artists, such as Amanda Palmer, now use online crowdsourcing to produce their work.

With crowdsourcing, you will need to create a short video (called an "ask" video) in which you pitch your project. If you don't have technology know-how, be sure to find someone who can help you. Just ask around! Kickstarter and Indiegogo both charge a percentage of the funds raised. Kickstarter also has two major limitations: 1. If you do not reach your goal, you lose the pledged funds. 2. Kickstarter pledges are perceived as an investment in the entertainment industry and not a donation toward the arts, and are therefore not tax-deductible. So, if you were to pledge $20 toward a project on Kickstarter, you might end up receiving something like a t-shirt for your pledge. This is actually viewed as a commercial sale. With Indiegogo, you are making a donation, even if there is no promise of a gift (such as a t-shirt, etc.). Also, with Indiegogo your project receives the donations instantly, and while you have a goal, you are not penalized for not making it (Indiegogo refers to this as "flexible funding").

TIME TO ACT AS ARTISTIC DIRECTOR

So, you have sponsorship and a proposed budget; you are raising funds, and you have a space. Now, it is time to use the money you have raised (or, are raising) to put together your creative team.

According to the *American Association of Community Theatres*, an artistic director can be defined as the person "responsible for conceiving, developing, and implementing the artistic vision and focus of a theatre company" ("Artistic Director"). His or her duties include hiring the director, designers, technical director, staff (front of house and backstage); "Acts as a spokesperson for the organization's artistic purpose via speaking engagements, public and social appearances, and, as requested, at fundraising events and solicitations;" and "Fosters the development of good relations with other cultural organizations by participating in meetings and joint activities where appropriate" ("Artistic Director"). Furthermore, the artistic director is responsible for the treasurer's reports and activities. To be clear, the responsibilities listed here are for an artistic director of a nonprofit theatre company. You, however, will be the artistic director of a single play, which means you will not be relying on other parties to carry out most of these tasks—for example, as producer and artistic director of your show you will probably be managing your own financial records, rather than relying on a treasurer or accountant). It will be up to you to foster good relations with the community. You are writing for these folks, so you need to make sure they are aware of what dialogue you want to engage in via your production: social justice? Local concerns? Generational angst?

When hiring a director, make sure he or she is someone who understands your play and has a vision for the work as well. Something that is often difficult for playwrights to fully comprehend is that the director, designers, and actors are all storytellers as well. Each will have a voice in the production. If this is too much to handle, you have the option of directing the play yourself, but I sincerely do not recommend it. While there are playwrights who have found achievement in self-directing (13P's Julia Jarcho directed her own play, which we will discuss in the case study), by-and-large I have found that an outside set of eyes and ears find moments that are clunky, and also find incredible moments that I was not even aware existed! Furthermore, to wear all of the hats—director, producer, artistic director, writer—could prove to be too much, and the production will suffer. As writers, we spend an incredible amount of time in our own heads. Trust somebody to help you see your work in a new light.

Being a producer (and artistic director!) takes a lot of time, energy, and focus. Make sure you are working with people that you trust—people who excite you and are excited by you. Remember to be humble (after all, lots of folks will be working with you, possibly for free) and always keep your sense of humor.

PLAYWRIGHTS COLLECTIVES

There are a number of production-based theatre companies that have emerged over the past decade spearheaded by playwrights who are actively creating their own opportunities. As Suilebhan suggests:

> In many ways, playwrights' collectives are the antidote to a lot of things that have gone wrong with the regional theater movement. Instead of working as jobbed-in architects (or whatever metaphor you might care to use), we become real estate developers. It's an important difference, and it's one that resonates with the shifts we're currently undergoing in the arts. Our institutions are transforming from (in the words of Diane Ragsdale) country clubs into civic institutions; there's a renewed importance on direct engagement between artists and audiences. That's the exact sort of platform The Welders (and other collectives) are building: not to try to abolish more traditional institutions, but to offer a kind of "yes, and" alternative solution (Email to Author).

Perhaps the most celebrated (or at least, most visible) playwrights collective was 13P (2003-2012). 13P consisted of thirteen playwrights who banded together in order to produce one play written by each member. The company formed in 2003, and "imploded" following the production of the thirteenth play. I am going to offer a brief history here, but if you visit www.13P.org, you will get the entire story, as well as a step-by-step explanation of how they were able to produce their own work in NYC. To be clear, their approach is a bit different than a writer producing his or her plays every once in a while. Their mission was to create a production company that would cease to exist once the company had produced a play by each member. Something like 13P takes a lot of time, talent, and dedication to raising funds.

The playwrights involved with 13P were Anne Washburn (P#1), Winter Miller (P#2), Rob Handel (P#3), Gary Winter (P#4), Kate E. Ryan (P#5), Ann Marie Healy (P#6), Sheila Callaghan (P#7), Lucy Thurber (P#8), Julia Jarcho (P#9), Madeleine George (P#10), Young Jean Lee (P#11), Erin Courtney (P#12), and Sarah Ruhl (P#13). Each playwright acted as artistic director of his or her own play, meaning they were in charge of finding their own director, designers, crew, and space for their production. Maria Goyanes acted as the executive producer for 13P (meaning, she was in charge of finding funds). Let's spend a little time looking at 13P in order to consider how they changed the self-production conversation, and to learn how we can create our own collectives.

13P: A CASE STUDY

In 2002, Robert Handel met Madeleine George and Julia Jarcho at the O'Neill Playwrights Conference. They also met Winter Miller, who was working at the conference as a literary staff member. Rob Handel remembers:

> We were all talking and complaining about our lives as playwrights. I met Ann Washburn through Madeline George, and we came up with this idea of starting a company in order to demonstrate that for the price of doing a series of readings or workshops you could instead do a series of [basic] equity [showcase] productions on a small scale. We invited a bunch of people over [to Miller's apartment] to talk about it, and thirteen people showed up [two via phone] and it became 13P. It was a random group. There wasn't really any aesthetic unity. We were more interested in creating a producing model than anything else (Handel Interview).

Two key points worth highlighting are the lack of aesthetic unity, which tends to define an arts organization, as well as the notion that 13P was interested in becoming a production model, one that could be replicated by others. Anne Washburn remembers the excitement in the room when the company was being discussed. There was a moment when she, and the other members, realized the company would be a reality:

One of the most important things we did as an organization was to determine the order. At that meeting when everybody was there, we worked out the order we would go in. [...] There was something about choosing the order ahead of time which made it easier with going forward. Periodically, we talk to people who want advice in creating their own company, I tell them to make the order ahead of time so there are no worries about people chickening out (Washburn Interview).

The youngest member in the room was Julia Jarcho, who, at the time of my interview, was ABD in Rhetoric at U.C. Berkeley. Jarcho remembers:

I was in college when 13P was formed, and I was not in NYC, but I had met Rob and Madeleine at the O'Neill the summer before, and I had stayed in touch with them. And basically, they asked me if I would be interested, and I was like "yes, of course." For me it started with the conference call. [...] I was the youngest, and it was like these artists I respected were interested in asking me to join their club (Jarcho Interview).

The "club" was rounded out by Gary Winter, Sheila Callaghan, Erin Courtney, Anne Marie Healy, Kate E. Ryan, Lucy Thurber, and Sarah Ruhl, with Maria Goyanes acting as the Executive Producer. To be clear, 13P is not "against development," despite their motto, "We don't develop plays. WE DO THEM!," which can be found on their website and in their publicity materials (13P). Rather, 13P offers an alternative to the developmental readings that are not geared toward a production of a play.

The members of 13P agreed on two points: the first, each playwright would act as his or her own artistic director. Unlike many other theatre companies dedicated to a theme or aesthetic style, members of 13P agreed to allow themselves artistic control of their own pieces, without the pressures of a single artistic guiding principle (outside of a commitment to full production). Second, each playwright functioned as his or her own producer of the show, which involved finding a space for production, publicity, deciding whether or not to invite critics (Lucy Thurber decided not to for her production of *Monstrosity*), etc. Playwrights also hired their own directors and design teams. Finally, by using the Basic Showcase Contract, an AEA (Actors' Equity Association) contract available to smaller, not-for-profit companies in New York City, 13P was able to create a functioning production model.

The Basic Equity Showcase contract has pretty strict, though achievable, parameters. As described by Ralph Sevush, Esq., in the July/August 2009 issue of *The Dramatist*, producers using the code are "limited to 128 hours of rehearsal," which can be distributed "across five weeks" (Sevush, 52). The budget cap for a Showcase is $35,000, and if the producer uses a "Seasonal Showcase Code," the producers may schedule a production for a "six-week run," while ticket prices are set at a maximum of $25 (Sevush, 52). Furthermore, actors are to be given a food and travel stipend during the rehearsal process and run of the show. As the name "showcase" suggests, Equity does not recognize plays produced by the New York Independent Theatre (an alternative name to Off-Off Broadway) as "professional productions," but as opportunities to give actors waiting on professional work exposure to industry. What needs to be addressed, however, is that playwrights are not paid for their work under this model, and most of the staff is comprised of volunteers (Lyons, 21). Therefore, if the rest of the team is to be paid, the playwright-producer must be an excellent fundraiser.

Trying to raise between $20,000 and $35,000 is a daunting task. Handel found the answer in Jim Baldassare, a press agent who "made the press take us seriously," and annual fundraisers, spear-headed by Maria Goyanes, who also serves as the company's executive producer (Lyons, 21). The budget for 13P is approximately $90,000 a year (21). Handel has offered the following advice: "Groups inspired by our model should know that foundations and governments don't tend to give to new organizations" (22). Therefore, as Steve Lyons has suggested, producers who wish to follow the 13P model "need to develop a reputation and be willing to cultivate a relationship with each grant making institution whose mission is a good fit with your work" (22). Madeleine George attributes their ability to raise a budget (of approximately $90,000 a season) to Rob Handel:

> The key to following through to our promise was Rob's skill and persistence in fundraising; the fact that he had arts management experience; he was a development officer at Mark Morris Dance Company. He knew how to make a non-profit arts organization solvent. Out of nothing. Mixed with the producing [know-how] of Maria turned out to be a functional recipe (George Interview).

With each playwright, there was a different approach to the artistic director hat. In this context, the "artistic director" for a single play hires the director and design team, and works collaboratively with them in order to ensure that the themes and/or aesthetics for the particular production are cohesive. Playwright Gary Winter's role as artistic director was "standard," as he was "involved in the casting, involved with the director" (Winter Interview). Julia Jarcho, on the other hand, decided to direct her own work, a taboo in the playwriting world. However, "with 13P," Jarcho says, "nobody batted an eyelash even though they haven't done it before. That's an example of how incredibly gracious and easy to work with everyone was" (Jarcho Interview). While the merits of directing one's own work or working with a director can be debated, the larger point to be made is that there was no aesthetic unity, no hierarchy, and no indication that there was a way of creating works that is not appropriate, and therefore should not be done. As Jarcho says, "It has never been about forming an aesthetic identity, or a characteristic mode of work; but it has been about producing these 13 pieces" (Jarcho Interview).

What 13P offers is a plurality of approaches, from writers of different backgrounds with vastly different ideas of what theatre is, and what it *can be*, as long as it is *produced*. One of the most prominent playwrights in America is 13P member Sarah Ruhl, whose *The Clean House* was a 2005 Pulitzer Finalist, and whose Broadway debut at The Lincoln Center, *In the Next Room (or the vibrator play)* dealt with a topic that is taboo and earned high critical praise. Writing for *The New York Times*, critic Charles Isherwood offers the following after seeing the Berkeley Rep Production in 2009:

> Comical though the play's depiction of Dr. Givings' methods might seem, it is based on historical fact. The use of primitive vibrators to treat women (and some men) suffering from a variety of psychological ailments referred to as hysteria is well documented. But Ms. Ruhl's play is hardly intended as an elaborate dirty joke at the expense of the medical profession. Her real subject is the fundamental absence of sympathy and understanding between women and the men whose rules they had to live by for so long, and the suspicion and fear surrounding female sexuality and even female fertility (Isherwood).

In short, playwrights involved with 13P's "do-it-yourself" model have made an impact on the current state of American drama. Ruhl's incorporation of yesteryear's avant-garde writing has proven successful with audiences and critics (Handel Interview). As Handel suggests, "People felt comfortable with *The Clean House*, so the metatheatrical world is not scary [for audiences] at all. It's fun" (Handel Interview).

CREATING YOUR OWN PLAYWRIGHTS COLLECTIVE

As mentioned, Gwydion Suilebhan is a member of The Welders, a playwrights collective in Washington, DC. It is similar to 13P insofar as The Welders are a producing organization consisting of playwrights who act as artistic directors of their own work. I asked Mr. Suilebhan how The Welders came about, and he responded:

> We developed organically. There were plenty of conversations among playwrights in DC about getting together in various permutations to do… well, something. […] Those of us who eventually became The Welders started talking in earnest, as a group, and those conversations slowly became more and more formal, till we were meeting regularly and making elaborate plans. We spent about ten months laying the groundwork in secret, then went public with a bang (Email to Author).

The Welders differs from the 13P model. For instance, they do not have a delegated non-playwright-executive producer. Nor do they have an "implosion device." As Suilebhan says:

> [In early conversations]…there was plenty of interest in imitating 13P. Some of those conversations started getting more and

chapter ten CREATING YOUR OWN PRODUCTION OPPORTUNITIES

more serious, then eventually a few of us started to frame a new concept: a playwrights collective that wouldn't implode, but that we'd give away to a new generation of artists as soon as we were done. That simple shift—adding a layer of generosity to seizing the means of cultural production—got people genuinely excited (Suilebhan).

In other words, when all of the current members of The Welders have had their productions, they will keep the organization going for a new group of DC writers as a way of giving back to the community that has supported their work. This act of generosity may be one way to keep the American theatre alive and the American playwright creating.

So, are you ready to build your own production company/collective? Creating a company is a much larger task than producing a single play for a brief run; however, if you work with a group, you will have the benefit of not going alone on this journey. As with the previous chapter, I am going to suggest steps for creating a company based on my interviews with members of 13P, as well as my informal conversations and emails with Gwydion Suilebhan. Keep in mind, these are suggestions. There is no "fail-proof" way to create a company.

Steps:
1. Find other playwrights.
2. Choose an order.
3. Define clearly who will be serving as executive producer for each work.
4. Define the role of artistic director.
5. Brainstorm funding opportunities.
6. Consider your audience.

FIND OTHER PLAYWRIGHTS

If you are already part of a playwrights workshop, this is the place to start. If you're in a class, ask fellow classmates. If you live in a community of artists, put up signs on callboards, use social media; I'm tempted to say, "if you build it, they will come." My hunch is, if you ask, "hey, are there any other playwrights near me?" you'll be surprised by just how many there are!

CHOOSE AN ORDER

As Julia Jarcho observed, 13P felt "real" to her as soon as an order was chosen. So, choose your order. Choose it during your first meeting (where you, of course, will have donuts). Then, decide if you will "implode" or if you are going to attempt to create a sustainable model. The latter will be tricky and there aren't many examples to point to. This is an economic reality. If you decide you want a long-running company dedicated to new works, start by producing each member's play (singular) before moving further. The economy, I'm afraid, is not kind to the arts (it's really not kind to anyone). Please do keep this in mind as you move forward.

DEFINE CLEARLY WHO WILL BE SERVING AS EXECUTIVE PRODUCER FOR EACH WORK

Will the collective act as producer, as is the case with The Welders? Will one person be assigned, as was the case with 13P? Will each playwright act as executive producer for another playwright's show? Is there anyone in your group who has arts administration experience? These are valuable questions that must be discussed fully and early in the process.

DEFINE THE ROLE OF ARTISTIC DIRECTOR

In fact, make sure everyone is using the same vocabulary in order to minimize any unwanted surprises down the road.

BRAINSTORM FUNDING OPPORTUNITIES

Research grants offered through The National Endowment for the Arts and state arts agencies. Remember, if you are a new company, you will have more trouble earning grants. Don't be afraid to start an Indiegogo campaign and *ask*. I know it is not easy to ask for funds. At one point or another, I have asked each of my Facebook friends for donations. I usually ask for $3-$5 a person. Many don't respond, some respond with $3, and every once in a while, someone will donate between $500-$1,000. The only way you get a definite "no" is if you don't ask. This is hard. It takes courage because you have to make yourself so completely humble. There is also a stigma attached to asking for money—we might think of ourselves as moochers, as unworthy. Be humble, but don't self-deprecate. If you want your work in the world, you sometimes have to move outside of your comfort zone.

CONSIDER YOUR AUDIENCE

This really should be number one. Who are you trying to reach? What are you trying to tell them? What do you want the audience to do? As you discuss these questions, visit www.13P.org for inspiration.

A FAIR WORD OF WARNING

Starting one's own company can be daunting, so much so that you should really take some time before jumping in. As Suilebhan suggests, before starting your own company, you should "self-produce...possibly a lot" (Email). He continues:

> Being a member of The Welders means spending most of your time producing other people's plays, and that takes a great deal of skill and experience. [...] For too many young artists, starting a company is simply a shortcut to producing a favorite play, but that's like swatting a fly with a sledgehammer. If you like a given

play, produce it; if you like another, produce that; and maybe after a while you'll need a company to keep doing what you're doing. But a company needs a mission that's bigger than the artists involved, bigger than any given project. So take some time to develop a deep sense of what you really want to do as an artist, and why you think that mission is right for your community. Then, and only then, should you go for it (Email).

So, what is your mission? Whom are you writing your letter for? What can you as part of a playwrights' collective incite an audience to do? Can you see your company existing beyond producing your own work? Should you have an implosion mechanism? Are you looking to pass the company to another group of writers? Make sure you have a series of serious conversations where you can hash out your mission. As Suilebhan suggests, if you are hoping to produce only your own play, you really don't need an entire company. Focus on the single play. However, if you and a group of like-minded writers share the pioneer spirit and wish to engage as a collective, then be sure to spend some time with The Welders website, read their mission, and of course, read their plays to see how others have blazed the trail (www.thewelders.org/).

CONCLUSIONS ON SELF PRODUCTION

On February 8, 2011, I attended the "Self-Production Panel" with The Dramatists Guild of America, Inc., the open-shop union for playwrights. The conversation was moderated by Roland Tec, a producer and Director of Membership for the Dramatists Guild; with panelists Rich Orloff, Elyse Singer, and Kathleen Wornock, all of whom are "self-producers"; and Dianne Debicella, founding member of Fractured Atlas, Inc., a fiscal agency that provides independent artists and organizations with not-for-profit status. During the course of the evening, Rich Orloff suggested that playwrights need to produce with "an audience in mind" (Orloff). Whom do you intend to reach with your production? Why should this specific audience see your play? What will they gain? What dialogue will they participate in (through the act of theatre), and how will that add value (in the broadest sense) to their existence? Remember, a play is a writer's letter to the world and we need to ask ourselves, which members of the world are we trying to reach?

For a playwright to select an audience to whom to write his or her letter involves excluding some citizens of the world, as the answer "a general audience" is never satisfactory. In other words, Orloff asks writers to consider audiences-as-communities. There is a tremendous amount of responsibility when writing for (or with) a specific community. Quality control can be measured by how successful the writer is with engaging in a healthy (not necessarily easy) dialogue with the community-at-large. In the next chapter, we will consider the limits of self-production, and the larger questions of artistic fulfillment as a measure of success.

CHAPTER
eleven

ARTISTIC SUCCESS AND OTHER ODDS AND ENDS

SUCCESS

What is *success?* How do we know when we have achieved it? In the U.S., success used to mean a Broadway production. As Jeffrey Ullom notes when discussing the legacy of Jon Jory at the Actors Theatre of Louisville, host of The Humana Festival of New Plays:

> [Jory's] dogged determination to maintain the visibility of his festival helped playwrights by altering the perception of success. By no longer needing to go to New York [i.e., Broadway] for validation as a writer, the [Humana] festival changed the perception of what a successful playwright could be (163).

For many, success is now measured by achieving a full production at one of the major regional theatre houses. However, it is becoming more and more challenging to get a reading, never mind a production, at the regional theatre houses. Looking at the study *Outrageous Fortune* by London, Pesner, and Voss, we can see that there are only a few channels to these major houses, and most of them involve earning an Ivy League degree. This is one of the many reasons why I champion the playwright-led production model. So many plays die in development, and those that don't, often become works that are better read than produced (Dietz).

As stated earlier, many playwrights have already started forming their own companies, which has changed how we may view success as a playwright. A number of these organizations have achieved mainstream notice and productions (The Workhaus, for example, is now in residence at The Guthrie Theatre, a LORT/ regional theatre in Minneapolis, Minnesota). Other organizations, such as Playwrights' Commons in Boston, offer workshops geared toward the writer, as well as residencies which bring playwrights, directors, actors, and designers together, who are then "tasked with brainstorming and writing/designing/devising theatrical projects that would have been impossible to conceive of as individual artists" ("The Freedom Art Theatre Retreat for Emerging Boston Artists"). Playwrights' Commons provides local artists with the ability to think theatrically and create their own theatre.

While self-productions had been viewed as "vanity productions" during the latter 20th century, there comes a point when a playwright has to take control of the means of production in order to make sure his or her work is fully realized, or, in the case of the New York Writers' Bloc, to make sure that he or she can achieve artistic integrity through the communal act of theatre games (via the playwriting workshop geared to the writer). Because of the rise of playwright-led theatre organizations, the term "vanity" has slowly been pulled out of the discourse of American theatre production; however, is there any merit in that pejorative term?

THE PLAYWRIGHT IN CONVERSATION

On September 27, 2005, Keith Urban, a director and playwright, moderated a discussion that looked at the ways in which the "historic avant-garde, The Language Playwrights of the 1970s and 80s (Mac Wellman, Jeffrey Jones, Len Jenkin) and the classics influence contemporary playwriting" (11). The panelists included Anne Washburn (13P), Jason Grote (co-chair of the SoHo Rep. writers and directors lab), and Caridad Svich (Resident Writer at New Dramatists and the author of scholarly publications dealing with the work of Maria Irene Fornes). The conversation was published in *PAJ* and given the title, "Contemporary American Playwriting: The Issue of Legacy."

Although a number of discussion topics came up (rather quickly) over the course of the conversation, there are two key points that I wish to highlight here. The first has to do with the self-consciousness of the American playwright. That is, the American playwright is, in many ways, haunted by the English model of playwriting, and therefore in some regards, sits in the British playwright's shadow. As Svich articulates it:

American theatre, especially for the past 20 years, has been asking itself, "What is American writing?" Originally, American writing was imported. Early American works mainly copied British dramaturgy. Around the 1790s, there was the development of the Yankee character and the beginning of a theatrical vocabulary that was uniquely American. But even so, there has always been a tension between homegrown work and English models of writing. American theatre has a complex that it is not good enough. You can see it in the kind of work that is imported or translated. We have practically no access to the contemporary theatre, for example, of Spain, Argentina, Mexico, or Venezuela. We still are under the burden of the Brits. But the avant-garde helps us ask in its stubbornly resilient way, "Who are we as Americans? What is American theatre?" The foundation of American playwriting is ragtag; it is songs and scenes, sketches and tableaus. How do we take that history and make it speak to an audience? We want an audience to say, "That's mine," to feel they have indeed a sense of ownership about the work as audiences do in other countries (12).

What Svich highlights is absolutely essential: audiences want to "own," that is, culturally recognize what they see being performed on the stage. At the same time, playwrights want to *own* the right to tell the stories they wish to tell their audiences. "Ownership" relates to both the notions of democracy, as well as the "do-it-yourself" model. To be clear, "owning" a work is not the same as "empathizing" with a work: empathy is more in accordance with the Greek model of audience catharsis; rather, ownership is a recognition of an aesthetic that has a component to it which points to a "rag-tag" history, of a plurality of individual voices and ideas, that for a brief moment connects with an audience as a gathering of *individuals*, rather than as a coded "group" with a singular "group mentality" (12). You, as a writer, are creating an experience that audiences will own.

The second point is tied closer to this present study: over the course of the conversation, Grote suggests that the 21st century has seen a "general trend to emphasize a 'do-it-yourself' mentality as opposed to relying on institutions" (Urban, 17). This notion of the American playwright/individualist leads to a confirmation of "do-it-yourself," since you don't rely on groups or outside institutions. Indeed, taking the current pulse in the Off-Off Broadway community, Grote argues:

> We have this sea of well-educated theatre artists, either coming out of MFA programs or not, and at the same time, there is an institutional crisis. But rather than wait around for institutions to recognize us, we find ways to make the work. It is not a deliberate rejection of institutions, but a realization that we cannot rely on them. We have to create our own opportunities (17).

Because playwrights are creating their own opportunities alongside other theatre practitioners and students, they are creating their own success. This is not a "pulling yourself up by your bootstraps story," because the with playwright-led "do-it-yourself" model, the self operates within the structures of community, and in order for the self to be successful (artistically or otherwise), the community must be successful as well (in terms of artistic conversation, education, the ways in which the theatre companies address their needs, etc.). As William Demastes articulates:

> When Aristotle famously observed that humans are political animals, he was observing that humans are by nature social creatures. We aren't programmed to live or work in isolation, but rather need to live together in a community. [...] If Aristotle was right, then the city of the community is where we belong, and the more entwined we are with our fellow citizens, the better it will be for the health of everyone. [...] Unfortunately, this is exactly what our modern culture endorses, encouraging us all to stand "free," unencumbered, and on our own two feet. If the Greeks were right, this pursuit of independent living explains exactly why we find ourselves so discontented in this modern world of plenty. Simply put, we're applying all our energy and resources to pursuing the wrong thing: independence (*Spalding Gray's America*, 81).

Demastes is suggesting that we as humans can only be independent to a point. We need to be an active part of a community.

ARTISTIC FULFILLMENT OR "WHOSE HAPPINESS MATTERS?"

As insinuated earlier, there is some anxiety when we discuss the role of commerce in art. Something to keep in mind is economic success is not the same thing as artistic fulfillment. I don't want you to think they are mutually exclusive, but let's consider the Broadway production of *Spider-Man: Turn off the Dark*, directed by Julie Taymor with songs and music by the popular Irish band U2. The opening night was been pushed back five times, and the various injuries and mechanical difficulties that occurred with the production became fodder for critics and pundits. In a shocking move, a number of major publications reviewed the show prior to its official opening (June 14, 2011, after 180 preview performances, "the most in history" (Healy)). In his review for *The New York Times*, Ben Brantley writes:

> This production should play up regularly and resonantly the promise that things could go wrong. Because only when things go wrong in this production does it feel remotely right—if, by right, one means entertaining. So keep the fear factor an active part of the show, guys, and stock the Foxwoods gift shops with souvenir crash helmets and T-shirts that say, "I saw 'Spider-Man' and lived." Otherwise, a more appropriate slogan would be "I saw 'Spider-Man' and slept" (Brantley).

Brantley concludes, "'Spider-Man' is not only the most expensive musical ever to hit Broadway; it may also rank among the worst" (Brantley). The review is pretty damning (and hilarious). How can a Broadway show—the most expensive ever mounted ($65 million)—be so poorly produced and received? Julie Taymor is no longer at the director's helm due to its terrible reviews and seemingly never-ending previews.

Bono of U2 has agreed with the *New York Times* review. In an interview with ABC news, Bono said the negative review "might have been a little hard for some other people around here to take that, but we don't disagree with the *New York Times*. That's the sort of stuff we were saying backstage" ("Bono Agrees"). In other words, *Spider-Man* has not provided Bono or others involved with the project a sense of artistic success, even though the gossip surrounding the show has led to sold-out houses. *Spider-Man*, due to the word-of-mouth of the various disasters surrounding the mounting of the production, is destined to be a commercial success, even though it is a critical and artistic failure. Put another way, tickets sold because audiences wanted to be there when the next actor was injured.

If a Broadway production is not tantamount to artistic fulfillment, what is? If we can broaden the horizons of artistic success to include a *satisfying* production at a Broadway theatre, a LORT Theatre, a Small Professional Theatre, a community theatre, a high school theatre, a college theatre, a workshop with a theatre company, or a reading in a living room with friends and colleagues, perhaps the theatre will truly become decentralized, and the false binary of amateur/professional will be dissolved (after all, if "amateur" can be defined as "lover of," then aren't even professionals in a sense amateurs?). However, a question that needs to be asked is this: whose satisfaction matters? Is it the satisfaction of the playwright? The actor? The audience? The community-at-large?

The idea of "artistic success" is incredibly amorphous and subjective. Indeed, over the years there have been a number of approaches to identifying the artistic success of a given work. A.W. Eaton has viewed the historic territory of artistic success as being tied in with ethics. For David Hume, for example, artistic success is directly tied in with audience response and empathy, as "the relationship between ethical defects and artistic value frames things in terms of conditions rather than in terms of mere interface. A work's artistic success can depend upon the audience's agreement with its ethical orientation, and failure to meet this condition can impede the response required for artistic success" (175). Eaton tends to find Hume's account of artistic success reasonable, arguing:

> [...] works can have a variety of merits and defects that we must balance and weigh against one another when judging the work as a whole. In some works an ethical flaw of the sort at issue here might be peripheral to the work's overall aims and thus outweighed by meritorious features that remain untouched by the defect (176).

A work, taken as a whole including its defects and merits (by whatever criteria these two equally amorphous terms can be judged), can be artistically successful when agreed upon by an audience (those who are meant to receive the work) and the creator of the work (playwright). In short, artistic fulfillment can be achieved in the balancing act between the playwright and the playwright's *intended* audience. The artist has a responsibility to engage with his or her community, and this engagement is a key ingredient to artistic fulfillment. Or, as Eaton suggests:

> In those cases in which it has been established that a work's artistic success indeed depends upon ethically defective responses from the audience, this will present an obstacle to that success. Such a work contains the seeds of its own artistic failure (178).

While Eaton is writing about a specific work of art, I am more interested in the conditions of reception for a work of art. Rather than negotiate what is or what isn't "ethically defective," an artist should present a work with an understanding of how an audience may react to the work, and taking responsibility for those reactions (good, bad, or otherwise). A playwright should consider the conditions for reception, where a work is staged or read, the role of the audience, and the audience's expectations for the theatre (which changes from community to community). Not only will keeping the audience in mind aid the playwright with the notion of artistic success or artistic fulfillment, but it may also help with quality control. I am using the phrase "quality control" to suggest that even though a play has been written, it does not necessarily deserve to be produced and/or published.

SELF-PUBLISHING?

Before jumping into the self-publishing debate, it is important that we understand the difference between play publishing and play licensing. If you sign an exclusive contract with a play publishing house, the company will act as a licensing agent for the play. Your play will be listed in a catalogue, published as an Actors Edition, and made widely available for theatre companies to consider as part of their season. You will earn a percentage of productions and a percentage of the books sold. If you sign a non-exclusive contract—such as the contracts one would sign to have their work published in anthologies with Smith and Kraus, Applause, or with Indie Theatre Now (online)—you still own the rights to the performance of the play, but the publishing house agrees to publish your work for a percentage of the books sold or for a flat fee. Before you sign any contracts, make sure you are being offered a fair deal. One step you should take is joining The Dramatists' Guild of America, Inc., which is the open-shop union for playwrights in the U.S. Although they cannot represent you in any legal disputes, their business office can show you examples of legitimate contracts and offer advice from playwrights working in the field.

In the playwriting world, there is a large debate about the nature of *self-publication* (not just self-production), or pushing one's plays onto the web. Responding to the new wave of publishing on the web—through *LuLu*, *Production Scripts*, *Createspace* (on Amazon), or through personal websites—Jason Aaron Goldberg, the editor and head publisher at Original Works Publishing, asks, "whatever happened to the honor of being published? With all this self-publishing we've lost sight of that" (*playwrightsbinge*). Goldberg also makes another strong point:

> By diluting the quality of the material being published even further we continue to hurt and hinder the truly strong playwrights from being read and produced on a regular basis. Just because you wrote a play doesn't mean it should be produced, and certainly doesn't mean it should be published (*playwrightsbinge*).

Publication as a reward is more-or-less an American phenomenon. Outside of the U.S., plays are often published before they are produced. There are a number of independent publishing houses which do not require a show to have been produced prior to publication. Goldberg's point that the market may be diluted is valid, but on the other hand some excellent writers, such as Alex Broun and Mark Harvey Levine, offer their plays via websites. Both playwrights have enjoyed a number of productions, and have earned national and international awards.

On a personal note, I only seek publication for plays that have had more than one production. After the show closes, I often go back in to the script and make adjustments. Leonardo da Vinci once said, "Art is never finished, only abandoned." After I have had a production or two of a play, I send it with a query letter to a publisher. With that, I abandon the project and move on to the next.

The "big houses" for play publications and licensing are Dramatists' Play Services and Samuel French. In order to have a play published with either of these companies, you will need to have had an extended run in a major city with major press coverage. As of writing this book (2014), both houses no longer accept submissions from writers. You will need an agent, and trying to find an agent when you're a playwright is a nearly impossible task.

There are some play publishing companies that serve community and high school theatres (Dramatics Publisher, Heuer Publishing), there are some that serve multiple audiences (the excellent Next Stage Press is an example), and then there are some that are a bit more specific with what they are looking to publish (Original Works Publishing will not accept any plays that have not had at least two productions; furthermore, they will not accept adaptations). Some houses publish online (Heartland Plays is an example), and some will offer either print or online. Be sure to research the different publishing houses before you make your submission.

PLAY LENGTH?

A challenge to the 21st century writer is to discover just how much time a play needs in order for the story to be told. Can the story be told in ten minutes? Ninety minutes? Three hours?

Our definitions of a one-act play and full-length play have changed. Between the late 19th and early 20th centuries, most plays had between three and five acts. By the mid-to-late 20th century, a play would have two acts, with an intermission between acts. The first act would run a little longer than the second. By the late

20th and into the early 21st centuries, 60 consecutive minutes or more would constitute a full night of theatre. Because of this new attitude toward play length, the festival-length play has become quite popular.

A festival-length play runs 75-90 minutes. There is no intermission. Festivals, such as the New York International Fringe Festival (FringeNYC) ask for plays that do not have an act break for a number of reasons, but perhaps the most important is economic. If a play has two acts, it will run longer than a 90-minute play, and therefore, fewer slots will be available. Some fringe festivals ask for works under 50 minutes. Ironically, most regional theatres produce plays with an act break, also because of economics. Regional theatres, and community theatres, tend to make money selling concessions. If there is no act break, no concessions will be sold.

If you decide to write a two-act play, make sure you end the first act with a compelling question. You need to end in a way that makes an audience want to dive back into their seats. I saw a production of Steven Dietz's *Yankee Tavern* (2007) at Shadlowlands Theatre in Ellenville, New York. It was a terrific production—great set, great lights, a sensational cast—but the end of the first act did not ask any question. There was no cliff-hanger. The act simply ended. Whereas the first act featured a number of rich, philosophical debates; the second act became somewhat of an action movie. The contract from the beginning of the play had been broken. I would have been entirely satisfied if the play had ended after the first hour and ten minutes.

A great example of an act-one question can be found in David Auburn's *Proof* (2000). The play concerns a young woman, Catherine, who took care of her father—a mathematical genius and university professor who suffered mental illness—up until his death. A graduate student, Hal, has found a number of proofs which, to be honest, I don't quite understand, suffice to say that they could be of major interest to the larger mathematic community and the world. In the end of the first act, Hal claims that a notebook containing a number of the professor's writings prove that he was still a genius despite his mental decline, and that determining authorship of the notes would be of monumental importance. Claire (Catherine's sister) asks who found the notebook: Hal or Catherine? Hal says he did not find it. Catherine then states, "I didn't find it. I wrote it" (Auburn). I remember sitting at an outdoor café the first time I read this play. I could not turn the page to "Act II" fast enough. Seeing it in performance years later, there was an audible gasp from the audience. The play had them talking, asking questions, and wanting nothing more than to return to their seats. The question of authorship was made so compelling! Auburn demonstrates the perfect use of the act-one question.

The ten-minute play came into fashion in the late 1980s thanks to the Actors Theatre of Louisville's National Ten-Minute Play Contest. Originally developed as a way to meet new writers (think of a ten-minute play as a calling card for longer works), the ten-minute play has become its own legitimate entity. There are a number of ten-minute play festivals around the country, each with its own operating procedures and submission guidelines. Ten-minute productions are great resumé builders, and one of the best ways to get your name out into the world. If you are interested in writing ten-minute plays, be sure to look at the Smith and Kraus yearly best ten-minute play anthologies.

PLAY FORMAT

Believe it or not, there is no "industry standard" for formatting a play. There are some who will debate this point, but from what I have seen from the guidelines at Yale, Samuel French, The Actors Studio, The New School, HB Playwrights Foundation, The Dramatists' Guild Resource Directory, and various workshops around the country, there is no single format. The key to playwriting format is to make sure each page is equivalent to one minute. This means the stage directions are usually somewhat indented, and the names of the speaking character is centered over the dialogue, which is flushed to the left.

I can tell you what I do, but keep in mind there are folks who will claim that this is wrong, too! I use Microsoft Word. I set my margins to the 2003 standard (1" at the top and bottom, 1.25" at the left and right). For stage directions, I increase indents to the center of the page (3"), and they run from left to right. There is a space between stage directions and the name of the speaking character. The character's name is centered, and the dialogue appears immediately beneath the character's name running left-to-right.

On the pages that follow, I have included Molly Pease's play, *King of the Woods.* It was one of two plays by Ms. Pease selected for the KCACTF Region IV Festival in Roanoke, VA in 2014. This play moved onto the Nationals. I asked her if I could include the play in this book. Ms. Pease uses the format I learned. Again, there are different standards, but the key is to keep the character's name centered over the dialogue, and to increase the indent for stage directions. Take some time looking at The Dramatists Guild Resource Directory, and then look at the play on the pages that follow. Keep in mind that 1 page = 1 minute is a rough guide. This play runs at 10 minutes, even though it runs onto page 13. Make sure you have your play read out loud before you submit it.

One quick note: never use Celtx. The format is nonsensical: the pages are never equivalent to one minute of stage time—really, not even close; plus, the format is very difficult to read.

King of the Woods

A Ten-Minute Play

By Molly Pease

CONTACT:
[Withheld for Book publication]

CHARACTERS

Vernon: a cryptic old doorman who guards the entrance to the hotel.

Henry: a young, wayward man.

SETTING

The lobby of an upscale hotel in New York.

SYNOPSIS

A comedic thriller based off of the Greek myth "The Golden Bough."
Think "Lord of the Rings" meets Seth Rogen.

HONORS

Selected for Nationals at the 2014 KCACTF Region IV Festival.

(VERNON is discovered behind the hotel desk reading a newspaper when
Henry enters. HENRY wears a scarf and
large coat. He walks towards the el-
evator.)

                    VERNON
Woah— hey! Young man! You want to hang your coat on the coat rack?

                    HENRY
What? No— thank you— I'm just seeing my friend and then coming back
down.

                    VERNON
You'll freeze out in that snow if you don't let it properly dry. I put
the coat rack directly under one of the heating vents so it's like a
clothes dryer. Little secret you pick up after working somewhere for
over 40 years.

                    HENRY
Well, no offense, but the ceilings are a little high—

                              (Vernon comes over and takes off
                              Henry's coat a little forcefully.
                              He hangs it on the coat rack.)

Okay— well, uh, thank you. For that.

                    VERNON
Now it'll be nice and dry by the time you leave. You better leave soon
though because the weather channel said this snow's bound to turn into
a blizzard by tonight.

                    HENRY
Yeah... I'll keep that in mind.

                              (Henry starts walking towards the
                              elevators again. Vernon returns to
                              his newspaper.)

                    VERNON
                 (*Not looking up*)
Oh, the elevators don't work.

                    HENRY
What? Why didn't you say earlier?

                    VERNON
I was busy trying to make sure you didn't freeze to death! No, the
elevators haven't been working all week. Maintenance guy is coming in
tomorrow.

                    HENRY
How do the people who live here get upstairs?

                    VERNON
They have a code to get in through the back.

                    HENRY
Okay...

                              (Long pause. Vernon continues flip-
                              ping through his newspaper.)

What's the code?

                    VERNON
Oh, I can't give it to strangers.

                    HENRY
I'm not a stranger, I'm—

                    VERNON
                 (Ignoring Henry)
I know everyone who comes in and out of this building at any time day
or night. Haven't slept in 45 years. (laughs)

                    HENRY
Ha right... well I just started dating my girlfriend who lives in this
building—

                    VERNON
Girlfriend? I thought you were here to see a friend?

                    HENRY
It's kinda new, guess we haven't really talked about labels—

                    VERNON
Labels? Labels are what the doctors put on my diabetes

VERNON (Contd.)

prescription. That's the problem with you young people: you are so wishy-washy. Love can only happen at first sight. First time you see her is when you know. Though I guess you might be referring to *not* having seen all of her yet— (*laughs*)

HENRY

I'm going to stop you right there. Look... my name is Henry—

VERNON

I'm Vernon G. Buckswallow III. Nice to meet you Henry. You seem like a fine young man—

HENRY

It's great to meet you Vernon— Mr. Buckswallow. But (*checking watch*) I'm a little late to pick my girlfriend up. If you could do me a huge favor and buzz her for me, then she can verify that I'm not a thief or-

VERNON

Or a rapist. We get rapists here too.

HENRY

You *get* rapists— what? Never mind. Just— call her and she will confirm that I am not either of those things. Her name is Diana Woodland. I think she lives on the fourth floor, maybe the fifth, she says her neighbors are like these really noisy hippies that play djembes and chant at all hours of the night—

(Vernon shuffles through some paper files in his filing cabinet.)

VERNON

Woodland... Woodland... hm...are you sure it's not Rock-sea? We have a Roxie. Ha! Get it?

HENRY

No, that's not it, but that's very clever—

VERNON
(*Finding file*)

Oh! Diana, of course! She's been here almost as long as I have! She's practically part of the building!

                    HENRY
I doubt that— she's around my age. Could there be another
Diana—

                    VERNON
Brunette? About 5'6"? Eyes as blue as a newborn bunny? Has a menagerie
of pets in her apartment, which is...(*checks file*) 435C.

                    HENRY
Yeah! That actually does sound like—

                    VERNON
Tattoo of an arrow on her left upper thigh? Has a sort of airy quality
about her you can't quite place? Abides by virgin virtues though her
companionship suggests otherwise—

                    HENRY
Yup, that's right. You can stop describing her now. Especially the
last part, pretty sure that's not true.

                    VERNON
There's a lot that'd surprise you about that fuckin' whore—

                    HENRY
I'm sorry, but did you just call my girlfriend—

                    VERNON
I said fecund. It means fertile. It's a compliment.

                    HENRY
Okay... (*under his breath*) maybe before the invention of birth control. (*To Vernon*) Anyways, that's her. If you could just buzz her for
me.

                    VERNON
We don't having a 'buzzing' system in this hotel.

                    HENRY
You don't— you just let me stand here and listen to— you know what? I'm
just going to call her. I don't know why I didn't think of this sooner.

                         (Henry pulls out his phone and dials
                         the number.)

HENRY (Contd.)

Man... I can't get any service in here. Maybe if I go
outside—

VERNON

Oh no, the blizzard has gotten worse since you've arrived. You don't
want to go back out in that mess.

HENRY

Worse? It hadn't even started... *sigh*... Alright, well I've exhaust-
ed every idea I have, so can you please tell me how to get into this
building?

VERNON

Hmmm... it's very strange.

HENRY

WHAT? That someone is actually talking to the doorman?! (*Beat.*) I'm
sorry, that was rude.

VERNON
(*Laughing*)

Aren't you abrasive? Yes, that is quite odd. You know it was snowing
the day I arrived here as well. We didn't have elevators back then. Or
this technological security nonsense.

HENRY

Fascinating. How would you enter the building then?

VERNON

Everyone had keys. And the doorman, he had the master key to all the
rooms. Now, I have that key. See it, hanging back there on that hook.

                              (Vernon points to a key that is sus-
                              pended in space; its own light that
                              comes up when he points to it.)

HENRY

Are you telling me that key is the only way into this building?

VERNON

That key is the only way into this building.

                    HENRY
I want to speak to your manager.

                    VERNON
One second, I'll buzz him in.

                    HENRY
Thank you— you don't have a buzzer system.

                    VERNON
We do not have a buzzer system.

                    HENRY
Are you the manager?

                    VERNON
I am the manager.

                    HENRY
I appreciate you not doing a whole Monty Python routine there.

                    VERNON
I find humor ineffective in situations such as this.

                    HENRY
And what kind of situation would that be?

                    VERNON
A situation of life or death.

                    HENRY
Woah— Vernon, dude, I don't know what you think is going on here. But
I'm not going to shank you over some key. No, thank you. I'll just wait
out back for someone to come in through the other door.

                    VERNON
No one's going to be coming or going in this weather. Tell me Henry,
what are you running from?

                    HENRY
What? Nothing, I came here to see my girlfriend—

VERNON

I'm well aware of the premise of your arrival. But how did you get here? (*Beat.*) I ran away when I was 16. It took me two years of traveling after that to make it this far north. When I got here it was snowing. Ain't never seen the snow before. I somehow stumbled into this hotel lobby to escape the cold. I can still remember the glowing letters against the steel gray backdrop: The Golden Tree Hotel.

HENRY

Yeah, you mentioned it was snowing before. Look I just want to—

VERNON

Go home.

HENRY

What?

VERNON
(*Slowly explaining*)

Why don't you just leave and go home. You've been mentally quarreling over this quandary at length and not once have you mentioned the possibility of leaving all together.

HENRY

What? It's... freezing outside... and I promised Diana... quarreling quandary? What, are you a troll guarding a bridge?

(Pause.)

HENRY

Sigh. I'm— uh— between homes at the moment.

VERNON

Your parents kicked you out?

HENRY

Do I look like I'm young enough to still be living with my parents? That's just insulting. (*Beat.*) Technically, it was my stepmom. They didn't like my change in major. (*Beat.*) As much as I'm enjoying this friendly chat—

VERNON

What did you change your major to?

HENRY

Religion. Not that it's any business of yours.

VERNON

How can you study religion? That concept is beyond the grasp of your mortal mind. Religion is all about power. The ultimate power. It plays with the hierarchy of the human soul. The only instance in which people willingly give control over to those with— more pristine morals. People whom are closest to the gods.

HENRY

You make it sound cold and political.

VERNON

Not political. Too much democracy in politics these days. Religion is a dictatorship. Pure and simple.

HENRY

I don't want to get into a philosophical debate right now. I just want—

VERNON

What do you want?

HENRY

THE KEY! I want the damn key!

VERNON

The key?

HENRY

I'm not repeating it.

VERNON

Upon the golden bough there lays
the promise of the future there
the kingship of the temple and
the worship of the goddess fair

HENRY

Excuse me? I'm sorry, but I thought I heard you speaking in rhyme.

VERNON

I should have known when I first tasted the bite of snow on the winter wind (*drawing a blade from the depths of his coat*) that someone would taste the bitterness of steal tonight.

HENRY

Woah, woah, woah, I am sorry that I made that joke about you rhyming and about you being an old, senile, saggy, troll— you are obviously very cognitively and physically capable for your age—

VERNON

Stop rambling. The time for incantations is over.

HENRY

Just tell me what you want and I promise I will get it for you.

VERNON

It's not about what I want, it's about what you want: the key. The last person to take that key down from that hook was me 40 years ago. It can only be taken along with the life of its owner.

HENRY

What does that mean? Does that mean you killed someone?

VERNON

I simply played my part in the hierarchy. For seventy years, he had waited knowing that one day someone would come and take his place. He lived always half awake and waiting. He was a shadow of a man who, by the time I got there, almost welcomed me as an angel of death. It will not be so easy for you. But that's good. The bond is stronger when you've won it properly.

HENRY

So you killed someone... over that key? The one up there? Why? Why would you do that?

VERNON

Why do we do anything? Power. The key has always been but it is only the representation of the place itself. The place was once on a grand hill overlooking a beautiful, lush orchard. Now, we have skyscrapers for temples. The buildings of ultimate power with loyal inhabitants. And although we've replaced stone with metal, you'll find that there is still magic in the material.

HENRY

How do you know all this... background if you killed the previous owner?

VERNON

Many people think that with knowledge comes great power but I assure
you, that is quite backwards.

HENRY

I don't want it. I don't want any of it. You can keep the key and I'll
go—

VERNON

Where? Where will you go? No home. No "labeled" relation-ship. A study
of faith rather than faith itself. You have nothing. You believe nothing. Who would notice if you died in that blizzard?

HENRY

I think I'll die faster in here than out there.

VERNON

Yes, I assure you it will be quite fast.

                    (Vernon runs at him, Henry dodges out
                    of the way.)

HENRY

Please, really, I don't want the key. I can just wait here until the
storm is over.

VERNON

The storm ends along with one of our lives. Nature has always been in
commune with the golden key.

                    (He dives towards Henry again.)

HENRY

STOP THAT! Stop with the cryptic lines and obvious death metaphors and
once and for all STOP TRYING TO KILL ME.

VERNON

I'm trying to get you to kill me.

HENRY

Why don't you just put yourself out of your misery?

VERNON

It's not misery, it's just time. And I can't break tradition.

                    HENRY
What if you do? What if no one succeeds you?

                    VERNON
What?

                    HENRY
That's how this works right? Someone kills the doorman and then they
become the door—

                    VERNON
The Master of the Key.

                    HENRY
The Master of the Key— yeah. What if you just died naturally?

                    VERNON
Then The Palace would die with me. Everything would be thrown into
chaos with no natural order.

                    HENRY
But this isn't natural—

                    VERNON
This is the purest form of nature. Alpha males take charge of their
pack until a younger male comes along and defeats the former leader.
Humans have a tendency to think we are above such rituals.

                    HENRY
I don't think that! I get it, we're all just animals. I just happen
to be the beta male—

                    VERNON
And that's what you want to be for the rest of your life? Don't you
think that there might be something to this key, this kingdom, to Diana?

                    HENRY
What does Diana have to do with it?

                    VERNON
Everything. Thousands of men before you and I have killed for her.
Even now I am willing to threaten my own life.

HENRY

Threaten your life? I'm not the one waving a knife in your face!

VERNON

You're right. (*Tossing the blade between them.*) Choose: power or death.

HENRY

What if you're making this all up?

VERNON

Then it is also a choice of faith.

> (Henry turns his back to Vernon and buries his face in his hands for a second. He then takes a deep breath, straightens up and takes a step towards the door. Vernon takes a step and leans down to get the blade. On hearing this, Henry quickly turns around, grabs the blade, and stabs him in the stomach. Pulling the blade back out in one swift motion.)

HENRY

Oh my god. Oh my god, what have I done (*He drops the blade.*) Vernon?

VERNON
(*Sputtering*)

Keep the blade, that which has defeated your enemy possesses their knowledge. Upon the golden bough...

> (Vernon dies. Henry sits for a few seconds in shock. He picks the blade back up and pokes Vernon's body twice to make sure he's really dead. He then stands up and climbs on top of the desk. The key's light reappears. He uses the blade to reach out and spear the key ring on the tip of it. Lights fade as he lowers the key. *End of Play.*)

THE DRAMATISTS GUILD OF AMERICA, INC.

According to their website, The Dramatists Guild of America, Inc. is a "professional association of playwrights, composers, lyricists, and librettists" (Dramatists Guild). They are an open-shop union. Unlike screenwriters who sell their work, playwrights own their work; therefore, playwrights do not have the power of collective bargaining. Screenwriters belong to the Writers' Guild of America, Inc. (WGA) which is a closed-shop union. The upside of having an open-shop union is that playwrights have complete, artistic control over their work, whereas screenwriters do not. If a director is making choices that include changing lines in the script or changing a character's gender or sex, the playwright has the right to cease the production, whereas screenwriters are often surprised by what they see on the screen on opening night. (For a wonderful case-in-point, be sure to view *Shadows of the Bat*, the documentary extra on the *Batman* (1989) special edition. Screenwriter Sam Hamm fought against two of the major act-three plot points: Alfred shows Vicki Vale the Batcave; Joker actually killed Bruce Wayne's parents when he was a young man. Hamm's reactions to these changes are priceless.)

Should playwrights join The Dramatists Guild? Absolutely! As stated throughout this book, we need community. The Dramatists Guild is a community and guild members hold each other's interests dear. Be sure to pick up a copy of *The Dramatists Guild Resource Directory*. I am sure you will be convinced.

MFA OR PHD?

Another debate in the playwriting community has to do with the importance of academic degrees. These are very personal questions and tempers tend to run high when engaged in these conversations. Some writers feel that MFA degree granting institutions are factories; art cannot be taught, and those who have a natural gift are standing in the shadow of academic institutions that control the pipelines to mainstream success. Others have argued that MFA programs create networking opportunities while giving writers the time needed to write their plays. Personally, I had a terrific time at The Actors Studio Drama School at New School University (2000-2003). My instructors were deeply invested in my work and made me feel like a colleague, rather than a colleague-in-training. Furthermore, I was in a major theatre city! I attended plays every week and became involved with a number of other folks who were looking to take what we were learning in class and put it out into the world.

If you think you might want an MFA in Playwriting, you will need to ask yourself some very personal questions—why do you want an MFA? If the answer is to hone your craft and build networking opportunities, super! What are the best MFA programs that can help you accomplish these tasks? Do you want/need to live in a major city? Are these goals something you can accomplish at smaller institutions? (Some folks would rather attend an MFA program at a distance from any major city in order to have a clear head while writing; others thrive in a city environment.) If you are looking to earn an MFA in order to gain access to the mainstream, you might be disappointed. Plus, if you are not on an assistantship and need to pay out of pocket (or through loans), you could end up disappointed, broke, and jaded. Weigh all of your options as you move forward, and always ask, "why do I want this?"

If you decide to pursue the PhD in Theatre, you will be focusing on scholarship. While there are creative writing PhDs, there are very few PhD in Playwriting degrees. My doctorate is from a research-1 institution (Louisiana State University); the classes I attended were history and theory (though I did take two creative writing courses as electives). I can safely say that during the first semester of my doctoral work, I read more plays than I had in the entirety of my undergraduate studies. This is not to suggest that they didn't have us read a ton of plays in undergrad, rather to stress the sheer amount of work that goes into earning a doctorate. Learning about the different artistic movements in theatre history has helped shaped me as an artist, though that is more of a byproduct than a reason to pursue a doctorate.

Perhaps the most rewarding aspect of earning both an MFA and PhD is that I now teach full-time at the University of Georgia. My students teach me so much and inspire me to continue writing.

WHERE CAN I SUBMIT MY PLAYS?

NYCplaywrights.org, Dusty Wilson's The Official Playwrights' Page of Facebook, and Aurin Squire's blog Six Perfections all list submission opportunities. Be sure to follow the guidelines for each opportunity. Make sure your play "fits" before sending! These sites are regularly updated. For a complete list of producing theatres, agents, and other opportunities, be sure to pick up a copy of *The Dramatists Guild Resource Directory*.

While most playwrights do submit to calls-for-scripts (I certainly do!), most of my productions were the result of forging relationships with actors, directors, and artistic directors.

A case in point: I had written a play, *Donkey*. It had a short run with the Rose of Athens Theatre in Athens, GA. I had also been raising funds with a director to have a full, three-week run at an Off-Off Broadway space. We hit a number of snags on the way. For one, we didn't raise nearly enough with crowd-sourcing. We were researching grants when the director landed a residency at a name theatre. He gave me his blessing to carry on. Time got away from me: I knew I owed our donors a show, but I also knew I would not be able to dedicate myself to the full run we had originally planned. I brought the play and the funds to the Rising Sun Performance Company, and they produced the play as part of the 2014 Planet Connections Theatre Festivity. It ran six performances at The Paradise Factory on East 4th Street, and won three Planet Connections Awards. The reason I was able to get this play produced in the end was because I have a relationship with Rising Sun that dates over ten years. Whenever you're in a bind, go where you're loved! (See Chapter 12)

CONCLUSION

One of my favorite movies is Frank Capra's *It's a Wonderful Life*. Clarence, the Guardian Angel, reminds George Bailey (Jimmy Stewart) that no man is a failure who has friends. Your artistic success should be measured by the people you are able to bring together, who want to share their ideas, and who want to hear yours. Whether you end up having a regional theatre smash, or a quiet conversation in a living room with pages scattered around the coffee table, only *you* can tell when you have done something with your writing (and your life!) that is worthwhile.

CHAPTER *twelve*

GO WHERE YOU'RE LOVED

"Do what you love, and know that you love it." – Nicholas Mevoli, (August 22, 1981-November 17, 2013).

I have been writing and producing plays since I was 18. I had absolutely no idea what I was getting into. I had not realized, in those early days, that I was beginning a journey that would take me through the rest of my life (I figure I'll stop when I'm dead). I have had a number of victories and I have made a lot of mistakes. I have learned more from my mistakes. It hurts when something goes wrong, but that hurt is really the pain of growth. It is easy for me to say that now. If someone had said that to me early on, I would have picked up this book and hit them with it. Hard.

Perhaps the most valuable lesson I have learned is to go where you are loved. You will meet folks along the way who think you are the sun, moon, and stars. They might be attached to a nationally-known theatre. They might be a group of community artists located in a town that's barely a wide spot on the road. Life's biggest gag is it really does not matter.

Sure, it's wonderful to see your name on the marquee in a major city, but it is even more wonderful to know that a group of people—regardless of national visibility—are willing to join you. If you find a team that's willing to stick with you thru thick and thin, they become your family.

When I started going for my MFA at The New School (during its Actors Studio Drama School days), I self-produced a few of my one-acts in various festivals. I worked with director Dennis Wayne Gleason who introduced me to Akia Squitieri, the artistic director of the Rising Sun Performance Company, an Off-Off Broadway troupe which, at the time, had two seasons under its belt. We immediately hit it off. I became one of their resident writers and I am happy to say that our relationship continues to this day.

It is pretty incredible what happens when you become so deeply entrenched with a group of like-minded artists. You grow together, grow apart, and grow together again. In 2013, an actor in our company named Nicholas Mevoli passed away attempting a free diving record. He had played one of my characters consistently for just under ten years. We grieved together, celebrated his life. Many of us are now quite a long way from NYC (I am currently writing from Georgia), but we still consider each other family. When you create theatre, you create family. These people will love you, tell you when you're on the right track, and tell you when you're way off. Listen to them. And they will listen to you, too!

LAST BITS OF ADVICE

If you are serious about being a playwright, here is a list of things you absolutely must do:

1. Read plays. Every play. Popular plays. Lesser known plays. Plays of every length.
2. Know your theatre history. Know theatre and other art movements. Know western and non-western theatre.
3. Meet actors, writers, directors, and designers.
4. Direct, stage manage, act, and design shows.
5. Fall in love.
6. Always remember why you started taking this journey. What *incited* you to write?
7. Keep a journal (hard copy) of everything you are thankful for. Keep it for yourself. Add three things to your list every day.

Thank you for taking the time to read this book. I hope this has been a valuable experience. Feel free to write to me from my webpage if you have any thoughts you would like to share—any victories, any lessons you've learned from previous mistakes; anything you wish to share from your journey. Thank you for allowing me to share mine.

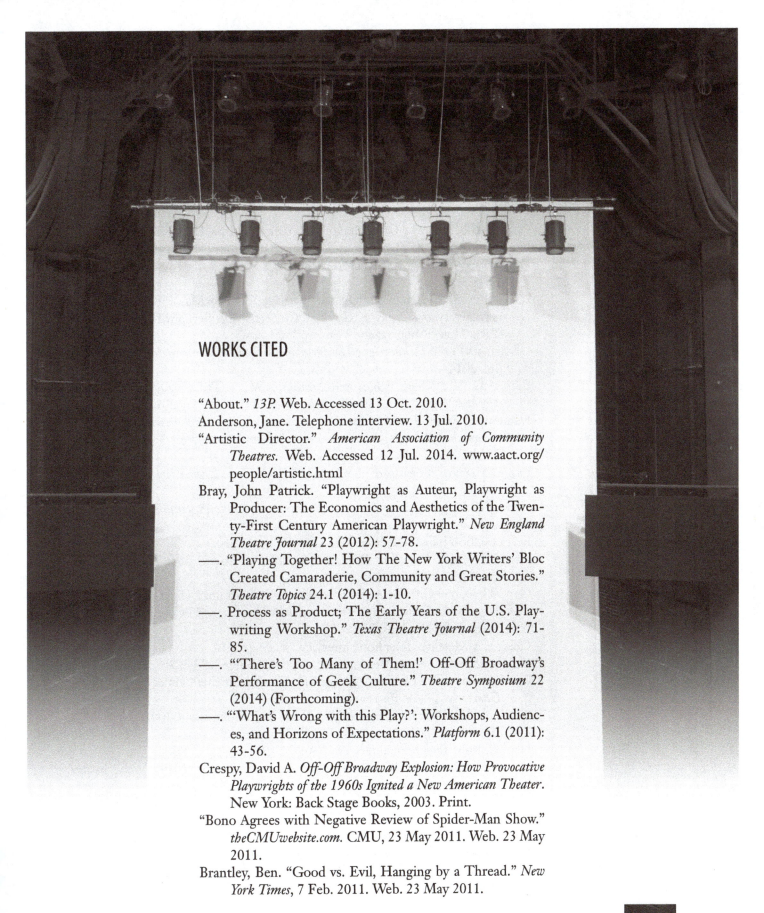

WORKS CITED

"About." *13P.* Web. Accessed 13 Oct. 2010.

Anderson, Jane. Telephone interview. 13 Jul. 2010.

"Artistic Director." *American Association of Community Theatres.* Web. Accessed 12 Jul. 2014. www.aact.org/people/artistic.html

Bray, John Patrick. "Playwright as Auteur, Playwright as Producer: The Economics and Aesthetics of the Twenty-First Century American Playwright." *New England Theatre Journal* 23 (2012): 57-78.

——. "Playing Together! How The New York Writers' Bloc Created Camaraderie, Community and Great Stories." *Theatre Topics* 24.1 (2014): 1-10.

——. Process as Product; The Early Years of the U.S. Playwriting Workshop." *Texas Theatre Journal* (2014): 71-85.

——. "'There's Too Many of Them!' Off-Off Broadway's Performance of Geek Culture." *Theatre Symposium* 22 (2014) (Forthcoming).

——. "'What's Wrong with this Play?': Workshops, Audiences, and Horizons of Expectations." *Platform* 6.1 (2011): 43-56.

Crespy, David A. *Off-Off Broadway Explosion: How Provocative Playwrights of the 1960s Ignited a New American Theater.* New York: Back Stage Books, 2003. Print.

"Bono Agrees with Negative Review of Spider-Man Show." *theCMUwebsite.com.* CMU, 23 May 2011. Web. 23 May 2011.

Brantley, Ben. "Good vs. Evil, Hanging by a Thread." *New York Times,* 7 Feb. 2011. Web. 23 May 2011.

Brecht, Bertolt. *Brecht on Theatre: The Development of an Aesthetic*. Trans. John Willet. New York: Macmillan, 1964.

Cardullo, Bert and Robert Knopf. *Theater of the Avant-Garde, 1890-1950: A Critical Anthology*. New Haven: Yale UP, 2001.

Castagno, Paul. *New Playwriting Strategies: Language and Media in the 21st Century*. 2nd ed. New York: Routledge, 2012.

Clark, Leroy. *Writing for the Stage: A Practical Playwriting Guide*. Boston: Allyn and Bacon, 2007.

Cohen, Robert. *Acting One*. 4th ed. New York: McGraw Hill, 2002.

Cook, Louise. "Snooping Exercise." Emailed to author. 22 Jan. 2014.

Demastes, William W. *Spalding Gray's America*. New York: Limelight Editions, 2008.

Dietz, Steven. "Developed to Death." *American Theatre* (May 1987): 42-43.

Dramatic Theory and Criticism: Greeks to Grotowski. Ed. Bernard F. Dukore. New York: Holt, Rinehart, and Watson, 1974.

Dramatists Guild Homepage. *The Dramatists Guild of America Inc.* Accessed 30 Jul. 2014.

Eaton, A. W. "Where Ethics and Aesthetics Meet: Titian's Rape of Eurpoa." *Hypatia* 18.4 (2003): 159-88. *Project Muse*. Web. 23 May 2011.

Edmonson, Brian. *Transforming Teaching and Learning with Active and Dramatic Approaches: Engaging Students Across the Curriculum*. New York: Routledge, 2014.

Esslin, Martin. "Theatre of the Absurd." *The Tulane Drama Review* 4.4 (1960): 3-15.

Euba, Femi. *Poetics of the Creative Process: An Organic Practicum to Playwriting*. Lanham: University of America Press, 2005.

Ferrante, Bob Jude. Telephone interview. 27 Sep. 2010.

Fisher, Teresa A. *Post-Show Discussions in New Play Development*. New York: Palgrave MacMillan, 2014.

Gerould, Daniel C. "The Americanization of Melodrama." *American Melodrama*. New York: Performing Arts Journal Publications, The American Library Series John Hopkins, UP, 1983.

George, Madeleine. Telephone interview. 19 Aug. 2010.

Goldberg, Jason Aaron. Message to PlaywrightsBinge. 15 Jan 2011. Email.

Graeme, Roland. "La juive. Jacques-François-Fromental Halévy." *The Opera Quarterly* 7.4 (1990): 155-163.

Gordon, Mel. *Dada Performance*. New York: PAJ Publications, 2001.

——. *Expressionist Texts*. New York: PAJ Publications, 2001.

Handel, Rob. Telephone interview. 9 Aug. 2010.

"Incite." Definition. *Dictionary.com*. Accessed 1 Aug 2014. Web. http://dictionary.reference.com/browse/incite

Jameson, Fredric. "On Neal Bell, Monster." *The South Atlantic Quarterly* 99.2/3 (2000): 371-375.

Jarcho, Julia. Telephone interview. 6 Sept. 2010.

Jenkin, Len. *Dark Ride*. New York: Dramatists Play Service, 1982.

Jones, Joni L and Iya Omi Osun Olomo. "Cast a Wide Net." *Theatre Journal* 57.4 (2005) 598-599.

Kaufman, Moises and the Members of the Tectonic Theater Project. *The Laramie Project*. New York: Vantage Books, Random House, Inc., 2001.

Kirby, Michael and Victoria Nes Kirby. *Futurist Performance*. New York: PAJ Publications, 2001.

Krasner, David. "I Hate Strasberg: Method Bashing in the Academy." *Method Acting Reconsidered: Theory, Practice, Future*. Ed. David Krasner. New York: St. Martin's Press, 2000 (3-39).

Healy, Patrick. "'Spider Man' Will Open on June 14 (So They Say)." *New York Times*, 11 Mar. 2011. Web. 23 May 2011.

Lehmann, Hans-Thies. *Postdramatic Theatre*. Trans. Karen Jürs-Munby. New York: Routledge, 2006.

Lerman, Liz and John Borstel. "Liz Lerman's Critical Response Process." *Contact Quarterly*. 33.1 (2008): 16-20.

London, Todd, Ben Pesner, and Zannie Giraud Voss. *Outrageous Fortune: The Life and Times of the New American Play*. New York: Theatre Development Fund, 2009.

London, Todd. "The Shape of Theatre to Come." *American Theatre Magazine*. Nov. 2001. Web. 9 Sep. 2010.

Lyons, Steve. "How to 13P." *The Dramatist* 11.6 (Jul.-Aug. 2009): 18-22.

Margulies, Donald. "Permutations and Dramatic Possibilities." *Playwrights Teach Playwriting*. Ed. Joan Herrington and Crystal Brian. Hanover, NH: Smith and Kraus, 2006. 22-38.

Marker, Lise-Lone. *David Belasco: Naturalism in the American Theatre*. Princeton: Princeton, UP, 1975.

Moore, Dawson. Message to the Author. 19 September 2013.

Moore, Dawson and Landford Wilson. "On Giving Feedback." *Last Frontier Theatre Conference 2011* (Program). Valdez: 2011. Moore.

Merson, Susan. "Teaching Philosophy." *SusanMerson.com*. 2011. Web. Accessed 23 Feb 2011.

Nelson, Richard. "Teaching Playwriting: A First Year." *The Dramatist* Sep.-Oct. 2006: 10-13.

Norman, Marsha. "Can Playwriting Be Taught?" *The Dramatist: The Journal for The Dramatists Guild of America, Inc.* Web. Accessed 21 May 2014. http://marshanorman.com/can_playwriting_be_taught.htm

Pease, Molly. "The King of the Woods." "Awards, Playwriting Selections." *KCACTF* Region IV. Web. Accessed 1 Sep. 2014.

Robinson, Marc. *The American Play: 1787-2000*. New Haven: Yale, UP, 2010.

——. *The Other American Drama*. New York: John Hopkins UP, 1997.

Spencer, Stuart. *The Playwright's Guidebook: An Insightful Primer on the Art of Dramatic Writing*. London: Faber & Faber, 2002.

——. "Spolin and Sills Laid Down the Rules. The Generations Who Came After Played By Them. That's How Chicago Invented Itself." *American Theatre* Jul.-Aug. 1990. Web. 7 Apr. 2011.

Schechner, Richard. *Performance Studies: An Introduction*. 3rd ed. Routledge: Abingdon, 2013.

Second State Theatre. "An Inside Look with the Cast of 'How I Learned to Drive.'" Online video clip. *YouTube*. 16 Feb 2012. Accessed 1 Aprl 2014. https://www.youtube.com/watch?v=cnnXVGME3xI

"Self Production Panel." *The Dramatists Guild of America*. Frederic Loewe Room, New York City, 8 Feb. 2011. Presentation.

Sevush, Ralph, Esq. "The Equity Showcase Code Revised." *The Dramatist* 11.6 (Jul.-Aug. 2009): 52.

Shklovsky, Viktor. "Art as Technique." *Vahid D's Official Website*. Accessed 1 Aug 2014. http://www.vahidnab.com/defam.htm

Smith, Anna Deavere. *Fires in the Mirror*. New York City: Anchor Books, Doubleday, Inc., 1993.

Smith, Erin F., Gary Steel, and Bob Gidlow. "The Temporary Community: Student Experiences of School-Based Outdoor Education Programmes." *Journal of Experiential Education* 33.2 (2010): 136-150.

Snyder, Blake. *Save the Cat! The Last Book on Screenwriting You Will Ever Need*. Studio City: Michael Wiese Productions, 2005.

Spolin, Viola. *Improvisation for the Theater*. 3rd ed. Evanston: Northwestern UP, 1999.

Suilebhan, Gwydion. Message to the author. 26 August 2014.

Sweet, Jeffrey. *The Dramatist's Toolkit: The Craft of the Working Playwright*. Portsmouth, NH: Heinemann, 1993.

——. Email to playwrightbinge. 10 Dec. 2010.

——. Message to the author. 1-8 Mar. 2010. Email.

——. Second message to the author. 8 Oct. 2013. Email.

——. "Innovators: Viola Spolin." *Dramatics Magazine*. Web. Jan 2011. 21 Jan 2011.

——. Telephone interview. 17 Mar. 2010.

——. Second telephone interview. 28 Apr. 2010.

Tec, Roland. Telephone interview. 25 Jan 2011.

——. "What defines an 'open submission' policy?" *Dramatists Guild of America e-Flash*. Message to the author. 25 Sep. 2009. Email.

"The Freedom Art Theatre Retreat for Emerging Boston Artists." *Playwrights Commons*. Web. Accessed 2011 Mar 30. http://www.playwrightscommons.org/main/Freedom_Art_Retreat.html

Ullom, Jeffrey. *The Humana Festival: The History of New Plays at Actors Theatre of Louisville*. Carbondale: Southern Illinois UP, 2008.

Urban, Keith. "Contemporary American Playwriting: The Issue of Legacy." *PAJ 84* (2006): 11-22.

Washburn, Anne. Telephone interview. 5 Sept. 2010.

Williams, Tennessee. "Production Notes." *The Glass Menagerie*. New York: Signet, 1987.

——. *The Glass Menagerie*. New York: Signet, 1987.

Winter, Gary. Telephone interview. 30 Aug. 2010.

Wright, Michael. Telephone interview. 1 Sep. 2010.

——. *Playwriting at Work and Play: Developmental Programs and Their Processes*. Portsmouth, NH: Heinemann, 2005.

——. *Playwriting in Process: Thinking and Working Theatrically*. 2nd ed. Newburyport: Focus Publishing, 2010.

Zaunbrecher, Nicolas J. "The Elements of Improvisation: Structural Tools for Spontaneous Theatre." *Theatre Topics* 21.1 (2011): 49-59.

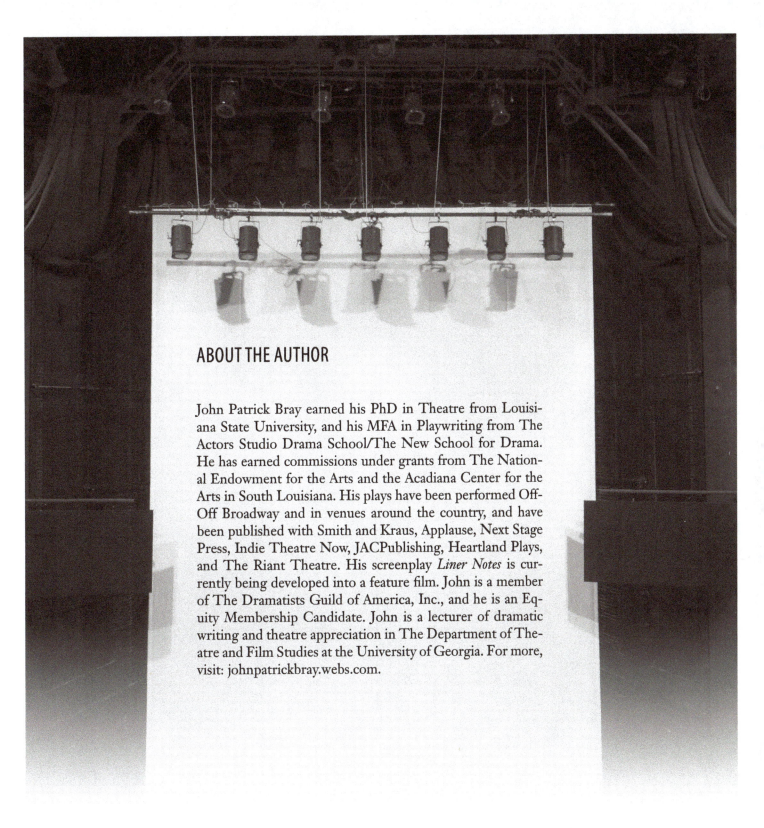

ABOUT THE AUTHOR

John Patrick Bray earned his PhD in Theatre from Louisiana State University, and his MFA in Playwriting from The Actors Studio Drama School/The New School for Drama. He has earned commissions under grants from The National Endowment for the Arts and the Acadiana Center for the Arts in South Louisiana. His plays have been performed Off-Off Broadway and in venues around the country, and have been published with Smith and Kraus, Applause, Next Stage Press, Indie Theatre Now, JACPublishing, Heartland Plays, and The Riant Theatre. His screenplay *Liner Notes* is currently being developed into a feature film. John is a member of The Dramatists Guild of America, Inc., and he is an Equity Membership Candidate. John is a lecturer of dramatic writing and theatre appreciation in The Department of Theatre and Film Studies at the University of Georgia. For more, visit: johnpatrickbray.webs.com.